Praise for Robyn Spizman and *Loving Out Loud*

"I got to know Robyn Spizman while overseeing the 9 o'clock hour of NBC's *Today*. She was one of the most conscientious and hardworking guests we'd come to know, which caused us to make her our go-to contributor. Robyn took creative control and made sure she knew the very last details about everything she spoke about. I don't think we ever had another guest contributor as concerned about making her segment absolutely perfect as Robyn. When I took over the fourth hour, with Kathie Lee and Hoda, Robyn became a frequent guest on that hour as well. It's rare you come across a person more concerned with content than Robyn. She is one of the very few who gets the job done from start to finish, adds her own signature, and on top of that, is always such a pleasure to work with."

— **Jo Mathisen**, cohost, Today Show Radio, SiriusXM, and podcaster, Podclair.com

"Robyn Spizman embodies community. She is a master connector and consistently engages with enthusiasm and kindness. Her 'how can I help?' approach makes it a pleasure to know her both personally and professionally."

— **Cheryl Kortemeier**, executive director, Corporate Volunteer Council of Atlanta

"Robyn Spizman is one of the kindest guests we have on the show. It's no wonder she holds the title of 'TV's Ambassador of Smiles.' She knows so much about so many things. It's a dream for producers."

director of creativ

"I have known Robyn for fifteen years. I can tell you first-hand that she radiates kindness! Through my breast cancer journey, marriage, and a baby, Robyn has been that friend who has been supportive and kind through it all. Her kind notes, messages, and words have helped influence how I treat others. My motto has become 'Spread joy and kindness like Nutella,' and that's what *Loving Out Loud* is all about. I have two young daughters, and I can tell you that each one of them will be getting their own copy of *Loving Out Loud*. Really, everyone needs a copy of this book because it is certainly life-changing! Thank you, Robyn! XO."

— **Cindy Simmons**, media personality,
www.cindysimmons.com

"*Loving Out Loud* helps us infuse each day with kindness and thoughtfulness and helps us build and strengthen connections with people who are important to us. A big thank-you to the 'gifting guru' who has gifted us this delightful guide to showing and sharing our love in the most meaningful ways."

— **Esther Levine**, founder of Book Atlanta Inc.

"Thank you, Robyn, for inspiring us to be the best version of ourselves. *Loving Out Loud* reminds us of the power each of us has to make the world a better place. Written in a way that is insightful and actionable, *Loving Out Loud* is a gem!"

— **Nadia Bilchik**, CNN editorial producer and author of
Own Your Network, Own Your Space, and
Small Changes, Big Impact

"I wish I had written this book. I am so glad that Robyn Spizman did."

— from the foreword by **Dawna Markova, PhD**,
cocreator of *Random Acts of Kindness*

LOVING
OUT
LOUD

Also by Robyn Spizman

Beyond Ritalin: Facts about Medication and Other Strategies for Helping Children, Adolescents, and Adults with Attention Deficit Disorders (with Stephen W. Garber, PhD, and Marianne Daniels Garber, PhD)

Do Your Giving While You Are Living: Inspirational Lessons on What You Can Do Today to Make a Difference Tomorrow (with Edie Fraser)

Don't Give Up…Don't Ever Give Up — The Inspiration of Jimmy V: One Coach, 11 Minutes, and an Uncommon Look at the Game of Life (with Justin Spizman)

The GIFTionary: An A–Z Reference Guide for Solving Your Gift-Giving Dilemmas…Forever!

Good Behavior: Over 1,200 Sensible Solutions to Your Child's Problems from Birth to Age Twelve (with Stephen W. Garber, PhD, and Marianne Daniels Garber, PhD)

A Hero in Every Heart: Champions from All Walks of Life Share Powerful Messages to Inspire the Hero in Each of Us (with H. Jackson Brown, Jr.)

Is Your Child Hyperactive? Inattentive? Impulsive? Distractible? Helping the ADD/Hyperactive Child (with Stephen W. Garber, PhD, and Marianne Daniels Garber, PhD)

Life's Little Instruction Book for Incurable Romantics: A Pulse-Quickening Collection for and about People in Love (with H. Jackson Brown, Jr.)

Make It Memorable: An A-to-Z Guide to Making Any Event, Gift, or Occasion…Dazzling!

Monsters under the Bed and Other Childhood Fears: Helping Your Child Overcome Anxieties, Fears, and Phobias (with Stephen W. Garber, PhD, and Marianne Daniels Garber, PhD)

Secret Agent (with Mark Johnston)

Take This Book to Work: How to Ask for (and Get) Money, Fulfillment, and Advancement (with Tory Johnson)

The Thank You Book: Hundreds of Clever, Meaningful, and Purposeful Ways to Say Thank You

When Words Matter Most: Thoughtful Words and Deeds to Express Just the Right Thing at Just the Right Time

Will Work from Home: Earn the Cash — Without the Commute (with Tory Johnson)

Women for Hire's Get-Ahead Guide to Career Success (with Tory Johnson)

LOVING
OUT
LOUD

The Power of a Kind Word

Robyn Spizman
Foreword by Dawna Markova, PhD

New World Library
Novato, California

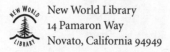 New World Library
14 Pamaron Way
Novato, California 94949

Text design by Tona Pearce Myers

Library of Congress Cataloging-in-Publication data is available.

First printing, August 2019

ISBN 978-1-60868-640-7
Ebook ISBN 978-1-60868-641-4

Printed in Canada on 100% postconsumer-waste recycled paper

 New World Library is proud to be a Gold Certified Environmentally Responsible Publisher. Publisher certification awarded by Green Press Initiative.

10   9   8   7   6   5   4   3   2   1

To my husband, Ed, who loves me out loud; and our children and grandchildren, who remind me to live, love, and laugh. You are my everything.

To Phyllis and Jack Freedman, who taught me the art of loving out loud. You'll live forever in my heart.

This book is also dedicated to you, my reader: Make the world a better place because you are in it. Be the reason someone feels *especially* loved today.

CONTENTS

FOREWORD

I wish I had written this book. I am so glad that Robyn Spizman did. We are living through a time when all the king's horses and all the king's men are shouting cruel things that are ripping apart the social fabric that holds us together. After watching the news every night, many people shrug and mumble "LOL," meaning either "This is so ridiculous it makes me laugh out loud" or "Lots of luck." Meandering through these pages, I found my breath going deeper, my shoulders relaxing, because it offers so many new and specific ways to grow forward *with* one another. It transforms "LOL" into "loving out loud," as it provides tiny threads to help mend and reweave that which connects us. It makes it possible for that habitual shrug to become a reach that can make us whole once more. Thus, *Loving Out Loud* is itself an act of kindness.

I'm thinking now of my father. I always wanted to hear him say "I love you." When I was a child, each time I asked if he did, he'd merely look away and tell me, "Here's a quarter. Don't tell your mother." When I was fifteen, I gave up asking. Then, years later, studying to be a psychotherapist, I learned to pound on pillows and scream, "I hate you, Daddy! I hate you." Two decades later, he was dying with Alzheimer's disease in Ft. Lauderdale, Florida. When I went to visit, my mind turned inside out. All I wanted was to express my love for what he had given to me. Kneeling in front of his shrunken body slumped in a favorite mahogany rocking chair, I said, "I love you, Daddy." His watery blue eyes reflected nothing. He hadn't heard a thing. He was locked behind walls I couldn't climb. Standing up to leave, an idea rose in my mind. I took out a five-dollar bill from my purse and put it in his wrinkled palm. "Here's five dollars, Daddy. Don't tell Mommy." He blinked, then looked directly up at me. In a clear voice I had not heard in years, he said, "I love you, too, sweetheart." It was the last thing he ever told me, the last lesson he ever taught me.

As human beings, we are not really equipped to create safety in isolation by burrowing in a log or hiding alone in a cave. The capacity to encourage, appreciate, and connect with one another is wired into our brains. We are meant to learn to widen our periphery, look beyond ourselves, and turn toward one another for safety. Your brain is the organ that learns how to do this. It is designed to be changed by your experience. Your mind builds your brain. Mental states can become neural traits. Where attention goes, connections grow. As you read the pages that follow, your attention will be guided toward small and specific gestures that enable you to bring light to people you know and care about, as well as those you don't know and *want* to care about. You will, in fact, be exploring the *how* of expressing and receiving love.

It took me decades to learn that love is not a noun or an object. It is not a thing you have or can lose, a fixed state you are in or out of. Love is a verb. Growing your ability to reach, speak, and act with love out loud will soften the numbness of your own heart and increase aliveness within and around you.

May all the king's horses and all the king's men read this book. Perhaps, after saturating your own mind with the possibilities it offers, you will even perform a random act of kindness and send one of them a copy!

— Dawna Markova, PhD,
author of *Living a Loved Life: Awakening Wisdom through Stories of Inspiration, Challenge and Possibility* and cocreator of *Random Acts of Kindness* and *Kids' Random Act of Kindness*

INTRODUCTION

SHARING THE BEST OF US WITH THE REST OF US

"I will not follow where the path may lead, but I will go where there is no path, and I will leave a trail."
— MURIEL STRODE, POET

It all began with a Post-it note and three simple words. *Good morning, beautiful.* It was meant to be a reminder from my husband that I am treasured. Neither of us is totally certain when it began, but I recall telling him I'd love that statement in lieu of a gift for

Valentine's Day…three little words, professed every day out loud. That would be the perfect present.

From that day forward, my husband has repeated the phrase "Good morning, beautiful." A handful of years later, he still tells me those words one way or another every morning. This tradition is a signal we are connected. His words have also popped up by my cereal bowl in the morning, affixed to my coffee cup, and posted on the bathroom mirror, leaving a trail of kindness. These little loving gestures, in turn, remind me of the power of loving him out loud, too.

I wrote this book to share the magic of loving life and each other out loud. To find the best in us and share it with the rest of us. It isn't just love in the romantic sense of the word, but rather the ability to profess out loud feelings we have when we adore, cherish, or care about someone or something. It's the excitement and passion we experience when we feel alive and connected. It's about being engaged with life and conscious of something greater than ourselves. It's about giving of ourselves because it's the right thing to do.

The phrase "loving out loud" refers to a way to live openly and without regret. It's moving from rapid-fire emoticons to thoughtfully emoting. It's recognizing the power of a gentler, spoken word infused with a generous spirit. When positive feelings are shared out loud, we give the gift of validation, inspiration, and love. And the best part? Someone hears us, believes what we said, and feels valued. That's a wow in my book.

In the pages that follow, you'll discover the secret to a life well lived. How every day we can wake up joyful, stay positive, and set a little love in motion. This reader-friendly guide begins with an understanding of loving out loud and how gratitude affects our lives. It is then divided into chapters focusing on each of your relationships, providing powerful ways for loving your significant other, family, and friends; raising kinder children; and valuing teachers, coworkers, your boss, and everyone in between. You'll learn creative ideas and insights to wake up kindness in your life while connecting better with the world around you. As you read, pause and reflect on each LOL (loving-out-loud) highlighted thought or deed. Get inspired by the LOL Snapshots, true stories of individuals putting loving out loud in action. And last, at the end of each chapter, activate the three things you can do today to jumpstart a kinder, more loving life now.

With this book's mission, together we have the potential to be a reservoir of goodness and a wellspring of kindness. Keeping positive thoughts locked up in our minds limits our ability to create more goodwill, and that's a waste. It's that simple. A good life is built one day at a time. Catch yourself or someone else doing something wonderful, and take notice. Slow down enough to connect with your caring and generous heart. Keep your words kind and your actions selfless, gracious, and accountable. That's what this book is about.

When we share a positive thought, the ripple effect is a vibration of happiness that has the potential to spark or strengthen a relationship. It puts a little pep in our step. Each of us can make someone else's day happy and influence their thoughts. Every day we can leave a reminder of our intentions and be a source of light to others, a blessing. By *being* the change we wish to see, we show others how we hope to be treated in return. Words go a long way, especially when they are shared out loud.

Kindness is contagious, but even more than that, kind words can be transformative if we believe and act on them. Quite a few luminaries agree on that. Alexander the Great, the Dalai Lama, Franklin Delano Roosevelt, Confucius, Ralph Waldo Emerson, Kahlil Gibran, William Wordsworth, and even my beloved mother and father. Add important studies done by leading psychologists and experts on matters of the human heart and mind, and it's clear that heartfelt, optimistic dialogue affects our well-being.

Sounds simple, but I know it's not always easy to express ourselves. It takes practice. A commitment. For negative thinkers, by digesting this book, you are changing a habit. For anyone who is not big on public displays of affection, you are about to take a risk and live large but can start small. We all long to be heard, valued, and understood and in turn receive empathy and appreciation. You'll be amazed by the benefits you reap as you follow the road map presented in this book to help you attract new friends, solidify your relationships, and inspire the best in yourself and others.

While kind words emerge from me with ease, many of us were not brought up being told how much we matter. If, on the other hand, we *were* raised with serial optimism, that's not to be confused with Pollyanna or maple syrup or wearing rose-colored glasses.

It's basic nurturing. Loving life out loud and sharing positive feelings captures a moment in time and preserves it. When I feel something kindhearted, I try not to resist the impulse to put it into words. I have realized more than ever that we can all be inspired to love each other — partners, children, family, friends — and the world around us *out loud*. When we exercise optimism and look for the good in others, we *find* more good. Writing down our feelings gives them a voice, but our *actual* voice, infused with kindness and generously disposed to others, has the unique power to spread hope and happiness.

I'm touched by people who never miss the opportunity to express themselves in uplifting ways. They embody the best of the human spirit and remind us of what a good life looks like.

When it comes to living and giving out loud, watch how when we lighten another person's load, we brighten our own world.

CHAPTER 1

START RIGHT, STAY RIGHT

Whatever your reason for picking up this book, it says something special about you. You care deeply about the relationships in your life or wish to get closer to others, be liked, and truly make a difference. You value kind words and might appreciate, or even need, gentle reminders to stay positive. Or, perhaps, you tend to keep feelings bottled up inside and want to learn how to let them out in a meaningful way without embarrassment or hesitation.

This chapter jump-starts your ability to love out

loud by charting a course to start right and stay right. Think of kindness as a marathon, not a sprint. Each step in the right direction enhances your life. We've all heard the adage "Start your day off on the right foot." It's true. We create a great day, one loving-out-loud step and moment at a time.

Let this book be your road map to a life well lived. It celebrates how the power of a generous thought and loving-kindness is transformative. I've seen it change lives, build better relationships, and make a person smile from the inside out. I've watched how parents and children have formed lasting bonds, and friends and family have reunited. By loving out loud and "saying" it forward, we can rest assured we are doing our best to be a blessing to family, friends, and those around us.

As you read on, be prepared to go be fabulous. Pause and ask yourself: "Am I ready to share my love and appreciation of life and others out loud?"

Loving out loud begins with the ability to say yes. To take a risk without delay. That means starting with a positive thought and building a new habit. Or even righting a wrong to get back on track. Negative feelings take up so much of our emotional real estate. Make room for more feel-good thoughts. Sharing your feelings might make you feel vulnerable and uneasy. However, the upside is that when you do, you will reap the rewards that loving out loud can manifest. Light up someone's life and brighten someone's day.

Let's get started.

LOL: Begin your day with an open heart and a positive attitude. Catch yourself or someone else doing something wonderful, and sit up and take notice.

Do Your Giving Out Loud

It's easy to enjoy receiving a compliment or positive feedback, but wait! When we love out loud and don't wait for someone else to do the giving, the opportunity rests in our hands.

Can you recall a time when you did something that started a "love [or even *like*] out loud" chain of events? Maybe you reached out to someone new to invite her for lunch, and before you knew it, you had a new friend. Or you handled a conflict or difficult situation with kind intentions, created peace, and built a stronger relationship. Sometimes it's as easy as being the one to begin or end a conversation with the words *I love you.*

In those moments, you *created* a loving-out-loud possibility and opened the door for someone to enter or even reenter. This idea works if *you* put it to work.

Try a little kindness. When you meet someone like-minded who shares some of your interests or whom you'd like to get to know better, here's a comment to open the door of friendship: "We have so much in common; I can really see us being friends." Project the good you envision, and hopefully the rest is history.

When we reach out to others first, rather than waiting for them to affirm us out loud, we give people permission to respond to us in kind. We have the power and innate ability to kindle a relationship in a surprisingly wonderful way. Consider: when was the last time someone's words or a deed truly had an impact on your life?

LOL Snapshot

When I think of people I adore being around, who have truly had an impact on my life, my dear friend of over thirty-five years, Bettye, comes to mind. Her cheerful disposition and ability to celebrate life despite her own family's tragic loss of a grandson to random gun violence are inspiring. Every month her family cooks hot meals and serves them to 180 homeless veterans and other individuals living under a downtown bridge. Bettye's healing comes from providing food to the needy, but even more, from providing hope. Selflessly she and her family connect with others to see how they can help further.

I asked Bettye how she gives back so effortlessly, despite her personal tragedy. She replied, "Pain can either challenge us or transform us. We turned our grief to giving. It doesn't take a lot of energy to help others or share a kind word.

"You don't have to overthink this," she explained, "especially if you are truthful. People are hungry for a kind word along with a hot meal. We serve both. When you share something you feel, like 'I think you are a wonderful person,' it comes out quickly because that thought just pops right up."

Bettye concluded, "We have so many sad people in

this world and people who, for whatever reasons, are over-looked. We tend not to notice them. All of us need a help-ing hand, kindness, and food for our souls."

> **LOL:** Choose an LOL role model. Think of some-one in your life (past or present) whom you ad-mire, who is great at sharing positive feelings, or who has lifted you up when you were around them. Make them your LOL role model. Think of ways to be more like them and spread kindness.

Love out loud across generations. My beloved mother felt that her own mother rarely said "I love you" to her. Everyone (including my mother) knew how much my grandmother Pauline loved her. While I pleaded with my grandmother to tell my mother she loved her, she replied every time, "Your mother knows I love her." Still, I persisted, "Grandma, you know it, she knows it, but she needs to *hear* it." I continued, "Tell her you love her, and say it often." Finally, she did. A few months later, my ninety-three-year-old grandmother passed away, but not without sharing her feelings out loud. Those three little words meant more to my mother than all the riches in the world.

Do not put kindness on hold. So many people go to their final resting place holding on to words that needed to be shared while they were alive. These words include *I love you*, *I'm sorry*, *Please forgive me*, and more. We all mean well, but we get too consumed with life's humdrum routines and many challenges, and shared feelings take a back seat.

We are here now and have an opportunity to reach out and show love. While a lot of time might have passed since you connected, hopefully it's not too late and there's a chance to rebuild a relationship or reunite with someone. Ask yourself, "What can I do today to create a better tomorrow?" or "What support or help do I need to positively and productively affect the relationships around me?" Work on understanding the steps you can take to move toward a more loving life.

> **LOL:** Have no regrets. Think of someone who, if they were not on this earth tomorrow, you would regret not having told how much you care about them. Do it now even if you think they know, it's uncomfortable, or it feels too late.

Master the Art of Appreciation

Loving out loud begins with an awareness of what's "right" around you. What's right in your world and in your life, versus what's wrong? If you look for the negative, you'll find it. Focus on the good and the positive.

In a conversation with me, Bruce T. Blythe, chairman of R3 Continuum, an international behavioral health firm, shared insights for staying positive:

In every case, happiness (and distress) comes from within. It's not the situation, but how I'm choosing to react to it. Happy people choose to be happy. Unhappy people dwell on unhappy thoughts. Think and do things that increase the likelihood of your happiness, even if they aren't a perfect "fix." Happiness comes from selflessness, not selfishness; giving with graciousness vs. expecting personal payback; self-forgetfulness versus focusing on "myself" and what I want. Happiness is not passive or self-centered. Happiness comes from active pursuits that make the world a better place because you were in it.

If you tend to be negative, Bruce suggests asking yourself, *Am I an awfulizer?* He explained:

Awfulizing (or catastrophizing) is an unproductive, negative thought process that makes life situations worse, or more awful, in one's mind than they are in reality. Ask if these negative (often complaining) thoughts support the well-being of others who are important to you. Focus on reactions and words that would be best for you and others. Think gratitude thoughts every day. Consciously acknowledge what you're thankful for, preferably at the same time each day, to make it habitual. Before going to sleep, think about or write down what went right today (no matter how trivial).

Appreciate the Positives in Your Life

Whether you are an introvert or extrovert, shy or out-going, it's possible to appreciate others out loud. The world needs introverts and extroverts. While this book is not designed to change you, we can all better relate to ourselves and each other. Consider this an invitation to notice the good in others. When you do so, your blessings will float to the top. Begin with bite-size moments of gratitude, and find ways to appreciate out loud the actions of others.

Everyone loves a compliment, which is a power-ful motivator to express your appreciation. We usu-ally think of a compliment as words that make us feel good ("You are such a fascinating person") or an ob-servation about someone's personality or appearance ("That shade of pink lipstick looks beautiful on you"). While compliments are certainly meaningful when sincerely given, go one step further and shift your per-spective from giving compliments to giving gratitude. Infuse your compliment with it. Think of your kind words as mastering appreciation, which is the mean-ingful, magnetic ability to make what you say stick. Re-cently my six-year-old granddaughter Dani overhead a compliment my husband gave me. She noticed how good it made me feel, smiled, and asked me if he went to compliment school.

The art of appreciation lets another person know what they are doing right, how much they matter, or what you notice about them that's special ("I really value the way you take the time to make sure my car tires are filled correctly; thank you for caring about my safety"). It ties the compliment into their actions and ices the cake with how you feel.

Your words of appreciation are like a boomerang returning kindness to you in a multitude of ways. When words are said without ulterior motive or the expectation of something in return, they come across as sincere and filled with good intentions. The receiver is more likely to believe them, as you do, and in turn your LOL acknowledgment affects them in a heartfelt way.

Personally, I appreciate the smallest acts of caring and a kindhearted spirit. A generous compliment, pure in motive, sincere in intent, echoes in my mind and keeps me afloat. Heart-to-heart compliments can turn someone's day around or start it off with a smile. That's remarkable stuff and highly underestimated!

How to Give an LOL Compliment

When sharing a compliment, infuse it with your appreciation for the person. Here are some ways to get in touch with that sentiment and validate others:

- Consider what you truly like (and appreciate) about the person: "I think you are one of the friendliest people I know. I'd love to be more like you."

- Think of things you admire about them: "I am in awe of the attention you give to details."
- Zero in on something that makes someone feel special: "Are you aware of what a thoughtful friend you are to me?"
- When focusing on physical traits, be creative: "When you wear that shade of blue, your eyes are sky-blue beautiful."
- Make observations about why someone is unique: "I absolutely love listening to you. Your stories are so interesting."
- Think of your words of gratitude as a thank-you gift: "My day is now perfect thanks to your thoughtful [birthday, anniversary, etc.] wishes!"

While at the post office, I thanked the kindhearted postal worker for his help as he advised me on the fastest way to send a package. He replied with a remark that really felt good: "You have such a generous spirit." I thought for a moment how to show my gratitude for his kind words, putting my stamp of approval on his attention, and said with a smile, "Return to sender."

LOL: When giving a compliment or making an observation about a personality trait you admire, put it in the form of a question. For example, "Have I told you lately how thoughtful you are?" Watch the smile appear on someone's face, just like magic.

LOL Snapshot

When Christine, a personable assistant at my hair salon, was in her twenties, her close friend Gavin gave her a compliment she still recalls word for word to this day, over five years later: "Christine, you sure know how to make people feel at ease." From that moment on, not only was Gavin's observation of Christine's outgoing personality sealed as a true compliment in her mind, but it also gave her renewed confidence. His words painted a picture of her strengths, and she went on to choose a career where she could put her people skills to work. Christine still reminds Gavin he gets the credit.

Show Your Appreciation of Others

Begin now. Think of a compliment you were given. What made it so striking that you remembered it and let it register? When words are positive and meaningful, they have the power to reinforce who we are at our core, or even how we wish to be perceived and remembered. Has someone commented on a color you wear that looks best on you? If so, what color was that? Do you remember the dress or shirt or outfit you were wearing? Do you wear that color more often as a result? How did the compliment affect you?

Remind and reinforce yourself. What are you good at? Think back to when you were little. As children we learn much about ourselves from what we are told. When I was in the first grade, the principal at E. Rivers

Elementary School displayed my artwork in the halls and shared her praise of my colorful self-portrait. I became an art teacher straight out of college, and somehow that little comment early on never left me and made me feel ten feet tall, even though at the time I was only six years old. Learn to acknowledge your talents and feel good about yourself. Equally important, notice the talents and skills of others, and acknowledge them. It goes a long, long way.

Hang around positive people. If you are around negative people, nonstop complainers, sour individuals who still grumble about the rain following the rainbow, that attitude is contagious. Those who treasure others are usually treasured themselves. Think of positive people in your life, and call them often. Make plans to see them. Positive people are priceless. Notice their traits and behavior. Share with them how their energy affects you and makes your day. Return the favor.

Be a gracious receiver. Next time you get a compliment, let it enter your heart and be thankful for it. Don't dismiss it; accept it graciously. Replay it to yourself as needed, and share it out loud to someone else who is deserving. Keep in mind that when you are given a compliment, someone took the time to share a kind word with you, and express your appreciation: "How kind of you to share such a lovely comment," or "Look who's talking; I'm in good company, and you made my day for sharing that." An expression of honest praise is the gift that keeps on giving!

> **LOL:** Give one compliment a day. Take a moment to look for a sincere way to share feedback with someone, and do so. You can give it directly to the person or go one step further and share it with their friend, parent, or sibling — or even their boss or spouse: "Do you know you have such a kindhearted wife? She takes such time and care with everyone she meets."

It's More Interesting to Be Interested

It's easy for some people to talk about themselves. We all love to be viewed as interesting and connect like-mindedly. We may talk about our lives, what happened that day, who we ran into, or our job. Add the kids, what we ate, where we went, and what we learned. Perhaps we tell a great story, a joke, or something we heard worth repeating.

All this, and more, certainly makes us very interesting. We think of it as sharing. We might be lively and fun to listen to, especially if we are not complaining (which is an entirely different subject). However, when we are a nonstop talker, others can't get a word in edgewise. If we return every subject to ourselves, we have work to do. If we monopolize the conversation, it's filled with "me, me, me."

It's reasonable to share what's on your mind, but when it comes to immersing yourself in "loving out loud" living, consider how you interact with others. The secret to connecting is being interested in someone else.

Try a little kindness. Watch what happens when you begin a conversation with a statement or question that shows interest in someone else and connects with what interests them.

After I buckled my four-year-old granddaughter Bella in her car seat after a long day at camp, she asked me with a big smile, "Ro Ro [that's what my grandkids call me], how was your day?" I did a double take in the rearview mirror. I looked at this precious child and smiled back. I was ready and excited to hear about her entire day, every precise detail, and she beat me to the punch.

> **LOL:** Just ask. Ask questions about others instead of endlessly talking about yourself. If you can't get someone talking, try inquiring, "What was the best part of your day?" Or say, "I'd love to know what you enjoy in life. Tell me about it."

Don't postpone kindness. Thinking lovely thoughts or even words that are reflective of the beauty of someone's presence on this earth and then not saying them out loud is a waste of a gift. Kind words take virtually no effort and are free. My father was often referred to as a "gentleman and a gentle man" for the endless kind deeds he did throughout his life, seeking nothing in return. I asked him one day at lunch, "Dad, why are you so good?" Without hesitating, he replied, "I don't know how to be bad." My dad was my superhero, and his power was kindness.

LOL Snapshot

I'm reminded of something I witnessed years ago while volunteering at a nursing home and someone there who didn't resist sharing a generous thought.

A gentleman visiting his infirm father noticed an elderly lady sitting at a table awaiting her own family. He noted how beautifully dressed this woman was and, after a second's thought, went over, bent down, and said to her, "Has anyone told you how lovely that outfit looks on you?"

The woman looked up, smiled, and replied, "Oh yes, my wonderful husband, who died last year, always commented when I wore this shade of lavender." The gentleman smiled at her as a warm surge of gratitude overcame him at that moment. He was moved that his words reminded her of her beloved husband. Clearly, they stirred memories she held close to her heart, which consequently touched his own.

> **LOL:** Have LOL radar. It doesn't take a lot, but it does take awareness, looking for ways to share kind thoughts and brighten someone else's day. Learning to be on the lookout for LOL moments can ignite a special day for someone else and rebound right back to you in return.

Give the Gift of Listening

While this book is all about loving out loud, words without corresponding action are just words. Words with sincere and honest intentions are *awakenings*. When we awaken that part of us or someone else and share these nonjudgmental, caring kindnesses, we get back even more than we give. We connect and feel closer. Words, once heard, enter someone's mind and become thoughts, which ultimately spur actions that can improve our relationships.

Sadly, when generous thoughts are dismissed and not shared, they are lost. But words with true intent and an authentic spirit have the potential to bring immeasurable reward. Words can motivate us and others to reach new heights or inspire us to achieve our goals and life purpose. It might sound lofty, but I'm convinced it's true.

Listening is just as important as talking. "Out loud" works both ways. First, avoid criticizing another person for not listening to you. That's a surefire way to shut someone down. Yet, how do we love someone out loud when we want to offer sincere feedback and say something constructive? If we wish not to hurt someone while telling them something for their "own good," our delivery, timing, and how we say it become critical.

Ask for the Gift of Listening

When you kindly ask someone else to give you permission to share your innermost thoughts or feedback, securing their attention sets the stage for a dialogue that structures a conversation in a more loving way. Psychologist Rick Blue calls this the "gift of listening" and suggests that you begin the conversation by asking for it when you want to share feelings that are sensitive or important to you. Once you in turn give the gift of listening, you can ask for it back. Without interrupting or blindsiding each other, you find a meaningful way to dialogue and share constructive feedback, which Blue feels is the basis of the best relationships.

Steps to becoming a good listener

1. Appreciate the other person for caring enough to share their feelings with you: "I love the way you tell a story. Thank you for sharing that with me."
2. Demonstrate attentive listening behavior by maintaining eye contact while you are talking, and stop what you are doing, if possible, to listen.
3. Do not interrupt or cut off their sentences because you think you know what they're about to say. Avoid talking over someone; learn to stop yourself, hold that thought, and wait while listening.
4. When the other person has shared their feelings, repeat what you heard, comment on it, or add to the conversation so you make it clear that you have listened and are interested.

Ways to Sit with a Negative Reaction to Deeds or Comments

When a comment comes your way that hurts your feelings, even to the core, sometimes you might not know how to respond. Instead of becoming instantly defensive, if you sit with it and determine what truth, if any, there might be, working through it will foster a more open relationship. If you examine your own actions, you can potentially learn more from the difficult feedback shared versus just the positive words. Both count.

We'd all love to sail through life with no storms or obstacles. However, if we work on our ability to hear what others have to say — the good and difficult — we're more likely to grow. An adage I love goes like this: "Don't go through life; grow through life."

Ask yourself:

- *What can I learn from this?*
- *Is there any part of this conversation that I am responsible for?*
- *What outcome would I like to see next?*
- *Do I need professional help in sorting this out?*

Make it safe for people closest to you to tell you the truth. If you are overly sensitive or unable to bear any conflict or face a difficult situation, it might be the best thing you ever do to work toward an understanding. Harboring hurt feelings deep inside gets no one anywhere. If you fall apart and overreact every time someone tells you something you find distressing or not valid, you will do the relationship more harm and yourself no favors. Remaining open to constructive feedback takes a willingness on your part. If you occasionally ask how you are doing, it might help you improve a relationship and allow you the ability to see how your actions are perceived.

Keep the goal in mind. When conversations go astray, think about what you want to accomplish. Being right is highly overrated. If you give up always being right, you'll build better relationships. Learn to agree to disagree and put your friendships and relationships first. That does not mean compromising your beliefs or values when someone says something negative or hurtful. Consider how important a situation is, and by giving up *being* right, you just might end up *doing* right and making more progress.

Know that it's not necessarily about you. It's not always about you, and once you view a situation as neutral and are able to understand the other person's perspective, you will be on the road to a more peaceful life with less drama and fewer hurt feelings.

> **LOL:** The gift of listening is something you can give and receive. Say, "May I have the gift of listening?" It's a two-way street that will strengthen your communication. Gift it often. Also, work on asking for feedback: "How am I doing this week listening to you?" When you learn to accept other people's comments, and avoid taking things too personally, it can sharpen your emotional acuity.

Just Remember This

Loving out loud begins with not missing the moments and details in life that count: acquaintances' names, family members' likes and dislikes, and friends' birthdays or anniversaries. When you start off organized, with an intention to honor a commitment or remember a specific name, date, or detail, it keeps you on track. Being able to recall this information requires writing it down or recording it to acknowledge its importance.

The first key to remembering is to slow down and pay attention. Capture names, dates, and details when presented, and register them. Fixing them in your mind is a concrete way to love others out loud. Exercise your recall often, and never take it for granted. Steve Ochoa, founder and president of Sharpen Your Memory, explained, "Using our five senses as often as possible, along with our sixth sense of emotion, reinforces our memory."

He offered these tips: "Repeat the data you wish to remember out loud to yourself, as hearing it reinforces the event. Writing it down so you can see it uses sight to help form the memory, and sometimes you can use the sense of smell to recall a date or occasion. Associating it with something you already have stored is the easiest way to help you remember it."

Here are some additional ways to improve your memory and LOL radar:

- Repeat a name out loud to remember it. I try to do this as a habit when I meet a new person. It's like crossing the street: *stop*, *look*, and *listen*. If you are introduced to someone named Karen, begin by saying, "Hello, Karen." Then: "Karen, it was nice meeting you." Repeat it, if possible: "Hope to see you again soon, Karen."

- Make an association by asking a question: "Karen, where are you from?" When she answers, take a mental picture of her. Think about something that ties Karen together with the location — perhaps a time you visited there — or associate her name with the place: "Hello, Karen from sunny Florida."

- Plant the name in your mind and add memorable details: *Karen is wearing blue and has on an interesting turquoise bracelet. She comes from Florida, where the sky and ocean are turquoise blue.*

- Put your memory to work! When you flex your memory muscle, you are strengthening it. Build a story that allows you to associate Karen's name with details: Karen *sounds like* sharing, *and we share a friend in common.* (The same concept holds when you leave home or another location. Make it a rule to scan your body. *Do I have my glasses, phone, purse, lunch* [etc.]? Try the "Head, Shoulders, Knees, and Toes" children's song or an acronym that keeps you checking yourself every time you leave a place.)

LOL: Want to remember it? Create memory backups with a datebook on your nightstand you look at daily, or virtual reminders with available programs that alert you electronically about significant dates and special occasions. Whether you use apps on your cell phone, online birthday alerts, or a virtual or desk calendar, it's important to lock and load these dates in advance to ensure you have them recorded.

Look for the Good...and You'll Find It

At the end of the day, by discovering and sharing your inner goodness, you have the innate power to shine your light and brighten someone else's world. We can all be serial optimists. Finding the silver lining in life is powerful. This book is about embracing and harnessing your kindness power within and then sharing the best of you with others.

Every day is an opportunity to look for the good. Even if we've fallen on hard times or encountered personal challenges, when we start acknowledging the little things we are thankful for, we identify the greater good in life. It takes time and a willingness to focus on what is right versus what is wrong — especially when life is chaotic or stressful — but new habits are possible, and loving ourselves and others can be accomplished.

LOL Snapshot

A laser-sharp insight came from Scott, a thirty-eight-year-old man with fragile X, a developmental disability that is genetic. He lives independently with support, works in the produce department at a grocery store, and participates in Special Olympics golf and basketball. He recently was honored with a "Power of One" award by a community organization for making a difference at the camp he has attended for many years. His mother, Gail, along with her family, was also recognized as a Point of Light recipient for dedication to community advocacy.

Gail asked Scott, "What does it mean to be kind?" He answered without hesitation, "It's when you are generous and helpful."

Gail added, "Scott learned early on that it's easy to sit on the right side of kindness. He has the same thoughts, feelings, and dreams as us all and is comforted by the kind gestures of others. He loves to be adored, respected, and recognized as someone who matters. My mother, Betty, summed it up best: 'You can never do wrong by doing right.'"

I'll never forget when I gave my daughter Ali the pretend title of our family CEO. That stood for "caring executive officer." Her job was to thank others for doing a good job, notice what they did right, and hire them! Ali noticed someone doing a great job, exemplifying excellent customer service, and she'd say, "You're hired for my Thank You Company!" One gentleman behind the register at a bookstore looked stunned when she said that. He replied, "I've been here for two years, and this is the first time a customer told me I was appreciated." He was truly touched.

In upcoming chapters, I will share the irresistible and kindhearted ways partners, parents, grandparents,

children, other family members, and friends communicate their feelings out loud and build better lives for
themselves and each other. You'll discover how to reach
deep inside you and get in touch with your inner kindness, making life more meaningful and magical.

Let today be the start of something kind. Get ready
to attract more positivity in your life. Miracles happen
every day, so let's get started!

> **LOL:** Look for the good, and you are more likely
> to find it. Say it out loud: "I believe something
> kind is around every corner." Loving out loud,
> coupled with a helpful attitude, leads to a fulfill-
> ing life. It's possible for every day to be kind —
> give it a try!

Three LOL Things You Can Do Today to Start It Off Right

1. **Add the "good" to your morning.** Create a good
    morning by thinking a positive statement and say-
    ing it out loud the moment you wake up. Or start
    your day by taking a deep breath before you get out
    of bed and envisioning something positive. At first
    you might just think it, but with practice, you'll be
    ready to announce it, hear your voice, and share it
    out loud with your family. You might feel awkward
    saying it out loud to yourself, but it sets the tone
    for your day, so go for it. Make your intention clear.

○ Try it: "Good morning, _____ [your name]. It's going to be a great day."

2. **Create and enjoy a morning ritual.** Every day I look forward to the smell and taste of my morning cup of coffee and breakfast. For years I've used the same coffee mug given to me by my friend Lorie. It reminds me to *slow down* and enjoy my morning moment instead of rushing through it.

○ Try it: "Ah, the first swallow of my coffee is so wonderful. I am so grateful for another day. Thank you."

3. **Make a kindness call.** Each morning before my mom passed away, I'd call her and wish her a very good day. I checked in like clockwork, and my day and hers got off to a great start. Now I call other family members or friends. Make a kindness call part of your "start right, stay right" everyday ritual as you check in on who needs to be bid a good morning and a good day. Or when you know someone has left work and is able to conveniently talk, call them. As you make loving others out loud part of your day, it will become a habit that gives *you* as much pleasure as you give them.

○ Try it: "Good morning, Ali. I just wanted to wish you a great day. I'm thinking of you today and am here if you need me."

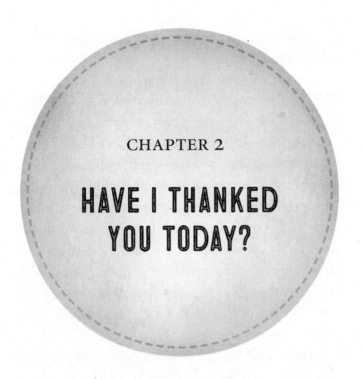

CHAPTER 2

HAVE I THANKED YOU TODAY?

Since I haven't thanked you yet today, let me do so now. I realize you could be doing any number of things at this very second, but you chose to read this book. For that I am truly grateful.

Having a mindful, kind attitude can change our view of life. I like to think of it as being a kindness "influencer," as with social media. Imagine together starting an LOL campaign of caring about each other. Watch what happens when you share an attitude of gratitude in your world and show appreciation to others out loud — it's electric and kinetic!

Albert Schweitzer summed up gratitude when he said, "Often…our own light goes out, and is rekindled by some experience we go through with a fellow-man. Thus we have each of us cause to think with deep gratitude of those who have lighted the flame within us."

When we appreciate someone and become that spark, a thank-you becomes a gift and lights us up. We all have so many people to thank. How we thank someone becomes part of our signature style of kindness. Studies continue to prove that the more we do for others, the happier we feel. There is a direct correlation. Cultivating kindness is a wonderful opportunity to uplift others as well as ourselves. When we turn our attention to noticing what we are grateful for, we bring out the best in ourselves.

That's what this chapter is all about. If you stop and think of all the people you know who deserve a thank-you, you'll be surprised to see just how many have an impact on your day, along with your life.

> **LOL:** Develop thank-you radar. Who are you going to thank? Acknowledge someone for something specific, versus just saying "thank you." Notice how when you look for thank-you opportunities, they appear right before your eyes.

How a Thank-You Can Brighten Your Life

There are days when we all feel down or blue. A thank-you "out loud" is a really nice way I know to shift a mood. It can begin with the power of a simple hello, showing your genuine delight and lift up another person, including yourself.

A kindhearted hello leads to friendships, new contacts, relationships, and more. You are not just breaking the ice but are igniting an opportunity when you take the risk to connect with another person and reach out *first*, sharing positive words or an observation. You create the possibility of making a new friend. In return, you are also seen as friendly, outgoing, considerate, engaging, complimentary, and interested. These good traits contribute to making a wonderful first impression.

LOL Snapshot

Frankly, my dear — I do give a thanks! Having attended Margaret Mitchell Elementary School (MMES) from second through seventh grade, I have always been proud that my grade-school alma mater was named in honor of such a wonderful author. Not only did Margaret Mitchell write *Gone with the Wind*, but she used to volunteer for the Red Cross in Atlanta with my grandmother Annie, of blessed memory, who brought her home-baked chocolate-chip cookies.

Our MMES class has stuck together for almost fifty years of reunions every five years. In the beginning of our get-togethers, our seventh-grade teachers, Mr. Pepe and Miss Ray, would attend. As the years went on and they got older and frail, my friend Gail and I went and interviewed them on video. Each reunion we thanked them for shaping us all, for caring, and for making our seventh-grade class the best year ever. Recently we attended Mr. Pepe's memorial gathering, and in our hearts we were grateful he knew how much he meant to us.

To this day, my old friends and classmates stay in touch and reach out to each other in many thoughtful ways. I think we all agree that kindness *is* elementary.

> **LOL:** Thank one person today. Celebrate your teachers, coaches, and those special individuals, past or present, who have made a difference in your life. Don't delay, as you'll never know when it will be too late.

Be Thankful Out Loud

The words *thank you* are universal in their ability to spread good feelings. It's clear that when we thank the people who touched our lives in little as well as powerful ways, we celebrate a part of life that validates each other.

Think for a moment:

- Who has helped you along the way in your lifetime?
- Who wrote recommendation letters on your behalf?
- Who took the time to teach you to ride a bike, read a book, play an instrument, hit a home run, play tennis, or cook a special recipe?
- Who makes your life easier or has come to your rescue?

- Is there someone who has been there for you through thick and thin?
- Do you practice saying "thank you"?

Every day there are opportunities around you, and when you seize them out loud, you build and increase your LOL radar. When you see someone in uniform who has served the country or provides safety or a public service, get in the habit of saying, "Thank you for your service." Here are some other ideas.

Make a Thank-You Date

A friend recently reminded me how special it is to thank others out loud with a scheduled "thank you" date or get-together. Every year, she takes her babysitters out for a thank-you lunch dedicated to expressing her appreciation. It makes her kids' caregivers feel special, and they make new friends at these dates, since they have so much in common. Whether it's a lunch to thank a teacher, breakfast to thank Grandma for driving car pool, a mother-daughter walk at the park, or a dinner with a friend who volunteered to help you, thank-you dates are memorable and a tradition worth establishing.

LOL Snapshot

Dr. Stephens drove to his clinic every day with an hour-long highway commute. Long before traffic apps were available to direct his route, he called the Department of Transportation (DOT) hotline. Upon getting to know the DOT ladies who worked there, he came to appreciate their efforts, and his calls made their day as well as his own. Grateful for their expert help, he decided to also send them a gift of candied pecans at holiday time. Often service providers don't get thanked, but this doctor wanted to acknowledge the DOT operators for their highway know-how, which kept him on schedule. The ladies were shocked, to say the least, since this was the only gift they had ever received at work. The next morning when he called in, they all got on the party line to share *their* thanks. This "roadway" thank-you was a two-way street.

Having written about the topic of thanks, love, and kindness for decades, I've discovered many clever ways to say "thank you," some that don't even use those words. For example, I loved it when a younger gentleman gave a handshake to an elderly coworker and said, "I want to shake the hand of the nicest person I've ever had the pleasure to work with. You are one generous soul."

I continue to marvel at all thank-yous that make us feel appreciated, but some hit it right out of the park. I'll never forget one I received that made me smile from ear to ear. It has stuck with me over the years as among the most touching thank-yous ever to warm my heart.

I sent a holiday gift to a friend of mine's daughter. As she opened it, her parents videotaped her reaction and sent me the thank-you video capturing her excitement. Her joy in unwrapping her present was off the charts. That was one gift that kept on giving joy!

> **LOL:** Don't postpone kindness. Today, try this exercise. Call someone who made a difference in your life and say "thank you." Sometimes they've done something little, and other times big. Perhaps it's been a while since you have seen an old friend who makes you laugh every time you are together. Reconnect. Who made you feel good about yourself and life? Who picked you up when you were down and needed a friend? People come in and out of our lives for many reasons. Even many years later, be thankful for those fleeting, tender moments, and do something nice in return.

Have an Attitude of Gratitude

At the end of the day, having an attitude of gratitude is simple. A wonderful habit to share with your family is to have a thank-you registry. Every time you feel thankful for someone or something, add it to the list. As you begin your list, you'll think of lots of things that are blessings, from food, to a roof over your head, to family and friends. Think of the pride you and your children will have when you tell someone they are in your family's "thank-you registry."

When I think about the kindest way to thank someone, I think about my mother and honoring her request to have the words *She tried* engraved on her headstone one day. She even put it in her will. My mother was very proud of how she handled life in spite of breast cancer, loss, and challenges. She always tried to welcome people, mentor other women to volunteer and get involved in the community, and look for the sunny side of the street. She never gave up and unfailingly believed in being kind. She tried, but even more, she succeeded.

We all have different ways of perceiving our worth on earth. David, a retired physician, shared with me how he wanted to be appreciated long after he's gone from this world: "I hope they'll say, 'Above all, he was a great listener.'"

Think of the many skills that embody the art of saying "thank you." Sometimes it's about giving advice, and other times it's just about listening and being heard. Look upon your life as an LOL blessing, and envision what you want others to recall when thinking of you. How will you be remembered and thanked?

Here are some of my favorite ideas that will summon a thank-you and add out-loud gratitude to transform your thanks:

- **Add words to your gift.** When I appeared in one of my first segments on a famous national talk show, I was asked to feature some of the best gift cards available to gift givers. I had an assortment prepared for the show, and said, "Give a gift card for a cup of coffee and tell someone you love them a-latte." At that moment, the show's host thanked *me* on national television in front of millions of viewers, which made my day. This wonderful response made me realize the power of words like *Thanks a-latte* or even *I love you a-latte*. I've found that clever words, when added to a gift, speak volumes.

- **Be creative!** Write a poem to thank someone, and read it to them in a toast at a dinner, gathering, or party. Whenever my husband, Ed, and I are invited to someone's house via email, instead of just saying "thank you," I will write a poem, a short little rhyme conveying an enthusiastic yes. Even if we must decline an invitation, I'll do the same. It's a fun way to get your message across. Or use an acrostic: take the sender's name and write, for example, "*Sally* stands for *Super, Attentive, Likable, Lovable You!*"

- **Present a gift for a gift.** While it's certainly not necessary, perhaps there are times when you'd like to reciprocate. When peaches are in season, my husband brings a few to friends and family. He's well known now for finding the juiciest peaches on earth and sharing them. Ed purchases them from farmers when they are at their best. He adores giving a "how-to" lesson on refrigeration and tips for how to eat them — to slow down, taking small bites — so as not to miss any of the freshness and delicious flavor. To thank Ed for his love-out-loud peach gifts, our friends Linda and Howard recently showed up with peanuts they boil with a special seasoning on them. Ed loved this gift for a gift.

- **Thank the boss.** If someone has served you with great attentiveness or done a superb job with customer service, a special thing you can do for them is ask to see their manager and thank the boss for having the wisdom to hire this individual. Recently I asked an employee who the boss was, and her immediate reaction was "Is something wrong?" I responded, "No, actually something is right!" Consider yourself an ambassador of thanks. You can do so much good by appreciating even the smallest of actions someone does to make your day.

> **LOL:** How will you sum up your life? I often think about my life and what I hope to accomplish along the way. My hope is that I have served as a blessing. At the end of the day, I want to be remembered as someone who didn't miss an opportunity to make other people feel special and loved. This goal is only accomplished day by day, so I remind myself to check in on what I've done each day to make someone else feel appreciated.

Be Specific with Your Thanks

A thank-you note is special, and even though you might have written a beautiful one, when you see the person, it is such a generous thing to thank him out loud. Also, if your note will take a little while to write (you're a bride, perhaps, or have a new baby), it's greatly appreciated when you call someone confirming receipt or leave a message to convey how excited you were and that a thank-you note will be there soon.

When expressing a thank-you, learn to be specific. Here's how and why:

- **Not specific:** "Thanks for the gift." Vague words like these will leave someone wondering whether you really even like the gift. What do you want that person to know? "Thanks for the gift" says very little.
- **Very specific:** "Hello, Laurie. I'm so happy I get to thank you in person for your thoughtful gift. I absolutely adore the keepsake you sent me. When I saw your gift wrapped so elegantly, I was so excited to open it. The gorgeous gold necklace with the beautiful pearls will always remind me of your generous heart of gold." Giving specific details about the gift or how it made you feel leaves someone knowing their gift was appreciated.

Ready, set, repeat. When you receive a thoughtful thank-you note or someone has otherwise expressed their gratitude, share the note or repeat the sentiment out loud with your kids and other family members present. I have a special box where I save thank-you cards and kind written words. Looking back at them occasionally reminds me of kind deeds I can do. If a teacher writes something nice about your son, share it out loud by calling Grandma or other family members. Watch your child's face when he overhears you reading the praise.

Sometimes you want to go the extra mile to ensure someone knows how much they are appreciated, even if you did not keep or like a gift, which does happen. When offering your thanks, focus on the way the gift made you feel. No one wants to fabricate false sentiments; instead, share your thoughts about the kind deed and your feelings for the person: "You sure made me feel special when you sent that sweater to me. It's no surprise you chose a gift of warmth; you are the warmest person I know. It's so nice to feel loved, and I am grateful we are related."

Share Your Thank-You Language

What is your "thank you" language? Developing your own style and way to communicate thanks is a personal thing. It can be done with regular calls, shout-outs on special occasions, kind deeds, sincere compliments, and even food. Feeding others, for many, is loving-kindness in action. My grandmother Annie put a little love and piece of herself in every chocolate-chip cookie, sweet tray, and special-occasion meal. Her dishes exuded love, and she showed her gratitude for family through the hours spent preparing everyone's favorites.

Bake Your Homemade Thanks and Make It Yours!

One way I love to express my thanks out loud to friends and family with good taste (buds, that is) is to bake a thank-you. I occasionally make my grandmother's apricot strudel that she lovingly taught me to prepare and drop it off to those friends and family members who I know love it. I have learned to master this one recipe, wrapping up a few pieces in a container with a sticker printed with the words *Baked by Robyn*. I am far from a great cook, but when it comes to baking this one delicacy, I've got it covered.

One of the things I enjoy most is when I bring my goodies over to someone's house or workplace. I've noticed the act of simply sharing something home baked speaks volumes. When I deliver my aunt's candy-bar brownies, I usually say, "Here are some brownie points for you for being so sweet to my family and me." Or "Here's a little treat because you're so sweet!"

My secret recipes for keeping a reserve of kindness on hand? Prepare ahead of time and store the bulk of the ingredients with a longer shelf life in your pantry. I also save some small containers that I might otherwise recycle so I am ready to gift my sweet sensations.

In case you are motivated, here are recipes for my grandmother's treasured strudel and my wonderful aunt Lois's sweet treat — the easiest dessert on earth to make, and a surefire hit — which she shared with me decades ago:

Grandma Freedman's Apricot Strudel

Ingredients:

2 cups sifted all-purpose flour

1 cup (2 sticks) butter or margarine, melted

1 cup sour cream (I use the real deal, but you can
    substitute low-fat)

1 medium jar (10 to 12 ounces) apricot jam
    (or any flavor works)

1 cup coconut flakes

1 cup finely chopped pecans, plus extra for top

Confectioners' sugar (for garnish)

Directions: Blend the flour and butter together, and stir in the sour cream. Chill for a few hours. Preheat the oven to 350°F. Divide the dough into four balls. On a lightly floured board, roll one of the balls into a 6 × 12-inch rectangle. Spread about one quarter of the apricot jam onto the rectangle, leaving an inch or so around the edges, and sprinkle about one quarter of the coconut flakes and pecans on top. Fold in the two 12-inch sides of the rectangle to meet in the middle, and pinch them together to form a log shape. Pinch the two ends of the log closed. Sprinkle some additional pecans on top. Repeat with the other three dough balls. Place the logs on an unbuttered baking sheet. (I like to line the sheet with parchment paper so the strudel does not stick to the sheet.)

Bake for about 45 minutes, or until lightly browned,

and be careful to watch it at the end to ensure it's cooked the way you like it. Remove from the oven and let cool. While it's still slightly warm, sprinkle the strudel with the confectioners' sugar. When cool, cut the logs into 2-inch slices. Freeze for later use, if desired, placing wax paper between the layers so they do not stick together.

Chocolate Candy-Bar Brownies

Ingredients:
Store-bought brownie mix (typically plus water,
    vegetable oil, and eggs, as specified on package)
2 large (7-ounce) chocolate candy bars
Crushed peppermint candy (optional)

Directions: Preheat the oven and prepare the brownie mix per the instructions on the box. Pour half of the batter into a baking pan (whatever size the box suggests) greased with a nonstick spray. This forms the bottom layer. Then break the candy bars into pieces and place them all over the top. Pour in the rest of the batter, covering the broken pieces of chocolate, and bake as directed. Remove from the oven and sprinkle the peppermint candy on top, if desired.

    Let the brownies cool. When the pan is cool enough to touch, put it in the refrigerator for an hour. When chilled, cut into squares and enjoy.

> **LOL:** Be creative when expressing your gratitude. Bake, craft, knit, sew, draw, paint, or shout it from the rooftops. Add a piece of yourself to the gift and make it by hand. Create your very own signature-style thank-you and make it memorable.

Pay Little Attentions Often

When you break down the art of saying "thank you," consider the little attentions you can pay. Notice these little things, and share them out loud.

- **Be aware of a thank-you voice.** The tone of your voice can say "thank you." Do you sound happy when someone calls you? Modulate your tone to reflect how pleased you are to hear from them. That's an LOL little attention.
- **Have a "Grateful for Girlfriends" luncheon.** Invite your gal pals to a themed lunch in your BFFs' honor. This luncheon can become a yearly tradition. Ask everyone to bring their favorite book, and be prepared to say why you loved it and have a book swap.
- **Go on a thank-you marathon.** Begin by thanking one person a day for a solid month. It might seem like a monumental task, but when you work your gratitude muscle, you'll be surprised how easily you build up a kindness habit. Consciously look for one new person — whether it's someone you know, a sales clerk, or the barista who gets your daily coffee order right — to thank every day out loud.

- **Be blessed out loud.** Consider what you are grateful for and say it out loud. Even if you are the only one who hears it, voice the blessing. You'll be better off for being aware of it. Whenever you feel like complaining, substitute the thought of that blessing. It's amazing what gripes from your "inner roommate" can be banished with a positive thought.

- **Create a thank-you jar.** Every time you are grateful, write what you are thankful for on a slip of paper and add it to the jar. At a special family dinner, read all the slips of paper. Or kids can create a thank-you jar for someone they adore, fill it with gratitude, and present it as a gift.

- **Make a thank-you kit.** It's easy to be prepared for thanking. Think of the people closest to you or those who truly brightened your day or had an impact on your life in some way. Have thank-you cards, stamps, stickers, and sentiments ready to share. I save greeting cards that touched me and enjoy looking at them often for inspiration. Personalize stationery for the kids, too, and make saying "thank you" fun.

- **Give a heads-up!** Whenever I find a heads-up penny on the ground, I repeat: "Find a penny, pick it up, and the rest of the day you'll have good luck." If you are with someone, give them the lucky penny. Or, if you want to jump-start a smile, leave it and a few more heads-up pennies scattered on the ground for other people to find.

- **Create a family "thank you" award.** Once a week (on Terrific Tuesdays, for instance, or Wonderful Wednesdays), give each family member a "thank you" award highlighting something you are grateful to them for. Did your daughter wake up with a smile? Did your son help clear the dirty dishes? Did your spouse call you when he was running late for dinner? There are endless little things worthy of recognition to reinforce the goodness.

If you periodically take a moment to consider what has touched you that you are grateful for, you are more likely to be able to get in touch with an attitude of gratitude. Then try spreading it until it sticks. Now we're talking!

> **LOL:** It's never too late for a thank-you. Being organized in advance, all prepped to express your gratitude, goes a long, long way. Get ready to say thanks!

Three LOL "Thank You" Things You Can Do Today

1. **Say thanks in your own backyard.** Begin sharing your thanks with people around you, from neighbors to local service providers to your bank teller. Think of it as a bubble or circle of kindness around you, and spread your gratitude. Change your narrative to include thank-yous every day. Be

a thank-you star, brightening your neighborhood during your daily routines.

2. **Give your time, talents, or treasures.** One of the most meaningful things I have done, which honors the memory of my parents, who were devoted to brightening the lives of others, is to connect with causes in my neighborhood and give back. By volunteering I am giving thanks out loud for my good fortune to live in such a wonderful community. Not only is it the neighborly thing to do, but it gives me endless joy to offer my skills and talents and be a part of something constructive and meaningful. Understand the needs of organizations near you, and see how you can fit right in. If you are friendly and good at greeting others, volunteer to staff the check-in tables at community events.

3. **Put gratitude on the menu.** Think of how saying "thank you" at a restaurant feeds our souls. Let's say you loved the food and the ambience, and your server did a fabulous job; of course you'd express your appreciation with a tip. However, LOL individuals go one step further. They learn the server's name, ask for that person upon returning, and even introduce themselves to the manager or owner and thank them if they had a great experience. The next time you go back, you have become a familiar face and are welcomed. Now, that's an LOL feast.

CHAPTER 3

INSPIRING YOUR PARTNER TO LOVE YOU OUT LOUD

A re you ready to inspire your partner to love you out loud? Do you wonder if there is anything you can do to enhance your love life? Perhaps you crave hearing kind words of appreciation and validation that you matter. Or on the flip side, you need help in sharing your feelings out loud with your significant other, which presents a challenge for you.

You might be someone who appreciates words that validate the depth of your loving spirit. Or you appreciate thoughtful actions and deeds above all else. But how do you make that happen? What can you do to effect the change?

We can't snap our fingers and make our partner love us out loud overnight. This book is not endorsing the goal of trying to change your partner fundamentally. It's not about transforming an introvert into an extrovert. There's no way to predict or promise the outcome of your LOL efforts, but I do know one thing for sure. How much you value and encourage positive communication and meaningful dialogue in your relationship is important. And what you say with your words and actions matters first and foremost.

Dialogue and communication are key to a fulfilling relationship. I have seen firsthand how the power of kindness and loving someone out loud and being true to your word can work wonders. When a partner feels truly treasured, it builds a bond of trust and strengthens a relationship. Loving out loud in all areas of your life is a process supported by actions that demonstrate your follow-through with your impeccable word.

While you might know what makes you feel loved, it's essential to understand what you *and* your partner in life value. It takes time and trust to build a common language of love, to create a loving relationship that makes each of you feel cherished and valued.

Your Loving-Out-Loud Language

We all have individual communication styles. Some of us are effusive with our feelings. Others prefer not to emote.

Love, as it's referred to in this book, is not just romantic in nature, though we associate it with a bond of the utmost affection. Rather, it's sharing feelings confirming we are treasured out loud. We all want to be valued for who we are and need a variety of relationships in life that are a reflection of that.

Think back to how you were raised. I come from a family that said "I love you" often. It was important for us to generously share those loving feelings out loud, including telephone calls daily whenever we were parted. In contrast, you might have had a very different upbringing and be someone who does not emote or even have an appreciation of it. You might have been raised in an environment that was protective of feelings, viewing them as not something to share. To you, it's foreign, isn't necessary, or makes you look needy.

Regardless of what type of family you came from, how you express love moving forward is your choice. You can love out loud and "be" the change you wish to see. If you are someone who keeps emotions to yourself, sharing those feelings becomes a gift as you meet someone else's needs. This awareness of how you affect another human being is a beautiful thing.

Look in the mirror and try reading the following words out loud: "I have permission to give and ask for the love I want today. I am worthy of being treasured and cherished." If you aren't comfortable speaking a loving word or it does not come easily to you, begin by thinking a kind thought.

*Questions for reflection to understand your
loving-out-loud language*

- Is it easy for you to divulge your feelings?
- Are you upset when you say something positive
  and don't hear the same sentiment repeated back?
- When you really like someone or something, are
  you able to share your feelings verbally?
- Do words spill out from you when you feel them?
- Do you say "I love you" or positive words often?
- When your partner shares positive feelings, do you
  easily respond in a reciprocal manner?
- Do you ever echo feelings back in an obligatory
  manner, or do you say what you sincerely feel?

Reflect on your own communication and first work
on loving out loud yourself. You are the only person
whose words you can think, shape, and express. Love
out loud freely without expecting something in return.

What Speaks to You?

When my father was dating my mother, he was working at my grandfather's office, where apparently there
was a lot of adding-machine tape. He penned a love
letter to my mother and mailed the entire roll to her in
a small box. She saved it for over sixty-five years, and
I inherited the love note along with a stack of love letters. I asked my mom why she saved the letters. "They
made me feel adored," she replied.

On a contrasting note, one remarkable and outgoing woman of my acquaintance has been married for thirty-five years and knows her husband loves her, but he rarely, if ever, shares his feelings. I asked her if after all this time there's anything she's ever done about it. She said she gave up years ago expecting a change, but it still hurts her. I suggested that for her next birthday, instead of asking for another piece of jewelry or a gift, she request a love letter. She willingly tried this, and weeks later as her birthday dawned, there was a letter of love from her husband sitting on her nightstand when she woke up.

She smiled and told me, "He got help writing it on the internet and borrowed a few lines from Shakespeare, but he made it happen. He likes quoting a few of the lines in the letter and seems more in tune to my need to hear these words. I think he actually likes being charming." The letter has become her most precious gift: "I read it every day, and it's my prized possession."

LOL: Notice your "loving out loud" language style and how you feel when you use it. Be aware of how it feels to love out loud and be loved out loud back in return. Try sharing one "I love you" a day, whether it be with your partner, your children, a pet, or yourself. The goal is to get comfortable stating positive feelings without fear of rejection, not hearing them reciprocated, or looking foolish. Be creative and celebrate expressing your feelings in a variety of ways with your own signature flair.

Why Kind Words Matter Every Day

Treat each day as the most important day you have, because it is. Imagine for a moment it was your significant other's birthday. You'd begin the day with loving wishes and end it on the same note. You'd put in a conscious effort to make the day special. *Every* day is a gift, and making the most of it builds a true love affair over time. The key is consistency and not just waiting for a special occasion.

LOL Snapshot

My dear friend's husband noticed she was feeling blue, as it was the anniversary of her mother's death. He texted me so I would know, writing that it would be helpful if I were to check in on her, but he asked me not to mention that he had informed me. I was so grateful to get that LOL request and immediately called my friend. She and I had such a wonderful talk, and it made *my* day that her husband reached out to me so that I could uplift hers.

Expressing love is not always easy but feels so good when you're on the receiving end. During a recent evening at a theater, a voice came over the loud speaker notifying everyone of the location of the exit doors and the theater rules. Signing off, the voice added, "And please remember this...I love you."

This went on over the entire week of the play's run, and smiles abounded. The audience agreed it felt so good to hear those words. It was no coincidence that people kept repeating this catchphrase to each other long after the final curtain fell.

Ask yourself what *you* can do to create a more positive environment for your partner and yourself. What messages do you share and enjoy hearing daily? If there is a serious issue in the relationship, are you getting help? Asking for and obtaining professional help is important.

Marriage counselors David Woodsfellow, PhD, and Deborah Woodsfellow, MPH, wrote a book called *Love Cycles, Fear Cycles*. In reference to the importance of kindness in your relationship, they shared:

> Kind, loving words are one of the easiest ways to try to create a love cycle in your relationship. It's a great idea to go first. Don't wait for your partner to start. Say some kind, loving appreciation or endearment to your partner. I like to do this every time I see my wife. If your partner responds kindly and lovingly, you two have just created a good moment. In a quality relationship you want as many of these good moments as you can get. And you want to stay in your love cycle as much as you can — where each of you acts kindly and makes the other feel good. That's the way to be happy and enjoy life together.

In the spirit of that thought, let's go first. We all have twenty-four hours a day, minus eight hours, give or take, for a good night's sleep. Here are some ways to love each other out loud throughout the day and evening:

Say "good morning." Every day a hello, "good morning," or note if your partner is still sleeping starts their day off on the best possible foot. Add the good back into the morning and share your loving daily greeting: "Good morning, beautiful"; "Hello, sweetheart"; "Love of my life, I hope you have a wonderful day. I will be counting the minutes until I see you again."

Give love taps. Love taps throughout our hectic lives perk us up. Whether you text an *ILY* (for "I love you") or a *C U soon*, it's fun to send little love notes throughout the day. One couple I know with three children has a lunch-break call date. It lasts only a few minutes, but touching base at lunchtime keeps them connected since their lives are so busy with the kids.

Ask "How was your day?" When you have a moment, checking in is an opportunity to catch up and stay connected. This show of caring makes a huge positive difference in your lives. Some days are less eventful than others, but staying in touch and listening to each other's activities can be both fun *and* informative and meaningful. You can also ask "What was your favorite or most challenging part of your day?" to spice up the conversation.

Say "Good night." At night, especially if you go to bed at different times, stop and tell your partner "good night." A good-night kiss or hug goes a long way. It ends the day on a positive note. Consider it a way to seal the day with a kiss.

Use terms of endearment. When asking your partner a question, add in a loving message or complimentary phrase. *How's the love of my life doing? What's my handsome lover boy up to? How's my sweetheart today?* Add your TLC to the conversation, and listen up.

Ask "Is there anything you'd like to share with me?" A couple I met enjoys asking for a report sometimes after a long, busy week where they both had a great deal of responsibilities. This "check-in, check-up" report keeps them both in touch and in sync with each other.

Give sincere compliments. Say something like, "You really impressed me today." Sharing a sincere compliment with your partner can make a big impact. Whether it's noticing their dedication to work or how their determination netted a big sale, share the quality that you admire with your partner. Be specific with your praise so they know what you valued.

Say "I'm so proud..." There are endless reasons to be proud of your partner, and when you say so, it's extremely meaningful. Consider expressing pride in particular personality traits and conscious acts of caring. Here are some examples:

- "I'm so proud of how generous you are with your time for our children."
- "I'm so proud of how you read a book to our grandsons online."
- "I'm so proud of you when you stop to pick up trash and help keep our community clean."
- "I'm so proud of how you conserve resources by not using plastic bags or straws because you care about the environment."
- "I'm so proud of how you love me with all your heart and make me feel cherished."
- "I'm so proud of what a wonderful father you are to our daughter."
- "I'm so proud of how patient you are with me when I'm under a lot of stress."

> **LOL:** Try saying "I love you" out loud every day, and offer your interest, attention, and praise. Make it a daily habit. Share your feelings in front of other people, and notice how good you feel when you do. The more you say it and mean it, the easier giving love out loud becomes.

Does Being Right Really Matter?

Join me in seeing the larger picture. Choosing positive, loving words takes discipline but lays the groundwork for treating someone else the way you wish to be treated. Do you point the finger when there's a problem and blame others? If so, it's time to try a new approach. As the adage goes, "You catch more flies with honey than with vinegar."

LOL Snapshot

A story illustrates my point: While at the airport on a trip to a foreign country, my husband forgot that he had nail scissors in his carry-on suitcase. He had to go back and check the item in order to get through security. While standing there for half an hour, I was getting frustrated, worried we'd miss the plane.

The security guard came over to me and said, "Madam, what's wrong?" I explained that I was waiting for my husband, and he advised, "Please don't be upset with him when you see him. He probably does not know this airport and is a bit lost." I smiled, calmed down, and proceeded to ask the security guard what made him choose to offer me such sage advice. He replied, "Every day I try to do something kind to help someone." I asked him what he'd done that he was proud of that day, and he responded, "I helped you." A few minutes later, he came back holding a laptop and asked me, "Is this your husband's?" Ed had forgotten the computer on the X-ray conveyor belt in his haste to go check the scissors, and the security guard had noticed it sitting unclaimed.

Not only did he rescue the computer, but he inspired me to greet my husband with kindness instead of irritation. I could see how much my husband appreciated my patience in that moment, and being right didn't matter.

Catch yourself and stop...

- Being critical, negative, and judgmental

- Blaming your partner and being impatient
- Pointing a finger over every little thing
- Needing to always be right and have the last word

Love out loud and start…

- Letting go of things that are not important
- Overlooking traits or little things that bother you
- Honoring each other's differences and accepting that we are all unique
- Viewing your partner's weaknesses as an opportunity to support them

Is It Truly Important?

What you *don't* say is as important sometimes as what you do say. You can't take words back, so try pausing before saying anything that's critical. Before you blurt out a comment you'll later regret, ask yourself, *Does this really matter, and is this life-and-death?* Most times, it's not.

How to avoid voicing a negative thought

- When you think something negative, consider something positive your partner does and let that cancel it out. In other words, trade the bad for the good, if possible.
- When you feel irritated that your partner is being inconsiderate, sometimes it's best to delay saying anything and notice if you are still bothered by the action later. Letting go of little things allows your partner to be themselves.

- Slow down. When we are in the heat of a moment, we say things we might regret. Our thoughts are moving fast, bundled with frustration, or spurred by a short temper. Breathe and notice if you are feeling tense. Slow down your thoughts and think things through.
- Give your partner a pass; a break; a way to make an error without your commenting critically, saying "I told you so," or placing blame. Keep the message of the song "Let It Go" in mind!

When You're Upset, Take a Break

When you're upset, irritated, or agitated by something your partner does, think for a moment: If you acted that way, how would you want to be treated? Would you like your significant other to have a short fuse and get upset with you, be impatient, or speak to you unkindly? Of course not. Not reacting to insignificant things that disrupt your day or grate on your nerves takes restraint and tolerance on your part. Imagine how empowering that can feel and how much space you give your beloved to not be so perfect all the time.

On the other hand, when things happen that are truly unacceptable, taking time to work out these issues is imperative. Don't start anything you don't want to finish, so to speak. Also, when it feels like your partner is crossing a line, verbally or otherwise, professional help is critical in order to establish personal boundaries and nip it in the bud.

Expressing Differences of Opinion

Agreeing to disagree sometimes is the best thing you and your partner can do. Harboring feelings accomplishes nothing except magnifying what you are feeling. We are creatures that need to feel understood.

When you express your feelings, timing is important. Before a big lecture or business trip is not the ideal time to tell your partner you want them to be more considerate.

To adequately address a topic, go for a walk and sit on a park bench or make a dinner for just you two at home, and focus on one thing. If you bombard your partner with too many messages at once, you will not be heard.

> **LOL:** Choose acceptance and kindness over being right the next time someone does something that's not important enough to get upset over. Treat your partner and others the way you'd wish to be treated were the tables turned.

Showing Up

Your presence is often the perfect way to let someone know you love them. If you have opportunities to attend special events where your partner is being honored, is speaking, or has volunteered, make it a priority to show up. Share your partner's interests and talents, whether it's simply watching them play tennis or attending a car show. Shared interests build engagement in each other's lives.

Ways to show up

- Find the way to your partner's heart through food. Discover what they love to eat that reminds them of someone who loved them. A grandmother's cookies. Mom's beef stew. Anything that evokes a feeling or supports your partner's needs and preferences — including healthy food choices, especially if they have dietary requirements or limitations — shows you care.

- Greet your partner's arrival with your undivided attention. Stop what you are doing, if possible, wait at the door, and greet your partner as if coming back from a long trip. Focus all your attention on a loving welcome home.

- Share a hobby or learn something brand-new together. From cooking to skiing to canasta, there are endless choices. It takes effort to align your interests, but it builds a stronger bond when you share these pastimes together.

- Maintain eye contact. I like to call it "Eye-love-you contact." How many times have you talked from another room or shouted across your home? If it needs to be communicated, say it face-to-face.

- Stop multitasking. All too often, we're looking down at our phones and talking to our partner at the same time. Model good listening skills by stopping doing two things at once.

- Hold hands, embrace, share a kiss, and remember the power of touch and the five senses. Show up by playing music that you both enjoy, and consider how to color your world with love out loud.

Just because. If you share your feelings only on special occasions, you are truly missing the opportunity to make your partner feel loved. "Just because" moments mean so much, because it's the little things that count. Here are some ways to share a just-because sentiment:

- Try saying, "Have I told you lately how great [kind, wonderful, generous, smart] you are?" Give your partner a truthful, kind compliment recognizing a specific trait.
- When standing under the night sky, seize the moment. Look at your partner and say, "I can't believe my lucky stars I am married to you."
- Give your partner a day off. Providing some space and taking on the daily duties is a gift of epic proportions. We all need a breather now and then.
- Hug your partner, share your feelings with a whisper, and don't immediately let go. They'll get the message.

Sharing your strengths. Loving each other out loud can often involve sharing your strengths. When my husband helps me with my technology challenges or teaches me how to set the thermostat, I consider it an act of love. When I help him select something to wear, it's my way of showing him how much *I* love him.

Barry was always losing his phone, wallet, and the list goes on. Ellen, his organized wife, viewed his constant disorganization as an opportunity to support her husband. She decided to help him keep up with his belongings, or at the very least double-check them before leaving a location. Instead of going on a daily treasure hunt for his things, she asked him, "Do you have your MAC pack?" (*MAC* stood for the "medication" he took daily; "aids," as in hearing aids; and "cell phone"!)

Knowing Barry was also liable to forget where he parked his car, which on one occasion was row 2175, his wife chimed in and said, "Sweetheart, I'm turning 75 but feel like I'm 21, thus 2175." Hours later, he recalled the car's location like a champ. Teamwork!

> **LOL:** Help your partner remember the little things that will make their day productive. Remind them of special dates they'll appreciate remembering and others will appreciate them remembering as well. Create your own reminder to reinforce the habit. Remember, it's the little things that mean a lot.

Starting LOL Traditions

Traditions and rituals make small moments *momentous*. Honor the traditions you have with your partner, and it's never too late to start new ones. These expressions of love build a lifetime of memories. Here are some traditions to include in your relationship:

Everywhere-you-go "I love you's." Vary how you say "I love you" to your significant other. When you are traveling, join me in this little love-out-loud tradition. I have said to my husband, "I love you in Australia," and wherever we travel: Norway, Italy, Israel, Hawaii — you name it. Recently, when we arrived at a beautiful seaside area, he was steps ahead of me, and before I could express my customary "I love you…" he chimed right in and said it first: "I love you in Sydney." It was music to my ears.

Love on board. When a plane takes off, my husband grabs my hand and squeezes it. It's a little "I love you" tap, but I know it means we're off on another adventure together. His hand holding also makes me feel secure and calm.

A toast to the most. Toasting each other is a beautiful tradition when you are having a glass of wine. Invent a signature toast that is worthy of repeating. One couple always announces "It's time to toast," and as they tap glasses, they both say, "I love you the most."

Sweet reminders. One woman carries a piece of sugar-free candy that her husband adores when she knows they'll be sitting for a long time or away from home. It's a little reminder that she loves him, and he appreciates it. If your partner has a sweet tooth, create an "I love you" message with a favorite candy: You're both on a roll with Tootsie Rolls. She's a lifesaver with Lifesavers. You're thrilled he popped into your life with lollipops. And of course, endless Kisses for the one you love to kiss.

"I Say a Little Prayer." Be sure to know your partner's favorite songs and musicians of all time. My friend Amanda, a dedicated fan of Dionne Warwick, shared with me that on her birthday, her husband set the tone for a lovely evening by having the beloved singer's music playing when he turned on his car, and he played all her favorite songs on the way to a special dinner. As another fan of Dionne Warwick, I can say that idea is also music to my ears.

"They're playing our song." While we were dining with friends at a restaurant, my husband got up and tipped the piano player so they'd play our song, the Beatles' "Till There Was You." That display of love made the evening truly memorable.

Picture this! Whenever our family is together, my husband offers to take a photo of the grandchildren and me. He makes the same offer when he sees a stranger taking a photo of a loved one. His generous spirit playing the role of photographer has captured dozens of couples and families creating picture-perfect LOL memories.

LOL: Just say it! Think of new and creative ways to say "I love you." *Je t'adore*. Say it in French, Spanish, Hebrew — give it a shot. Love is love, the universal language.

Feeling Safe and Secure

At the end of the day, feeling safe and secure is what makes many of us feel loved. These are actions and feelings, not necessarily words, but creating a loving and safe environment represents an invisible language of kindness at work. When we feel better about our surroundings, we also feel better about ourselves.

When we feel taken care of and take care of ourselves and our families, it's an expression of love and not to be underestimated. Knowing we are loved is important, but letting our partner know we value their safety and security is a life-protecting and potentially even lifesaving way to share love out loud.

All of us have fears, concerns, and thoughts that keep us from feeling safe and secure. While it might appear that a breach of security is a random thing, subject to chance, begin by concentrating on yourself and what is controllable. You might be fastidious about the little things, and your partner might be somewhat careless or absentminded. Consider what matters to you, write it down, and discuss it together. If you aren't organized, you'll find yourself nagging your partner or focusing on the negative too often. Create a loving language that shows respect for your private lives by ensuring appropriate security measures are taken.

"LOL Safety Checklist" Recommendations

- Lock the doors of the house. Agree on a protocol.
- Child- and pet-proof your home. Keep everyone safe.
- Remove hazards stored in areas that are unsafe.
- Check smoke alarms and carbon-monoxide detectors to be sure they are working and batteries are replaced as needed or on a schedule.
- Securely store credit-card statements, passports, and other sensitive documents.
- Do not leave important papers or belongings lying around the house in plain view or in visible areas in your car.
- Have checks conducted regularly, as advised, on your home's cooling, heating, and electrical systems; gutters; pipes; and so on. Be proactive.
- Update insurance policies (of all sorts) and wills, and place vital records in a vault or safe-deposit box.
- Make duplicates of keys to keep on hand just in case.
- Create a list of passwords and contact information of all service providers hidden in a book.

LOL: When your partner changes the batteries or replaces lightbulbs, acknowledge this with a "thank you." Don't miss the opportunity to show your appreciation for deeds both small and big. Taking care of each other is truly loving out loud.

Three LOL Things You Can Do Today for Your Partner

1. **Begin and end every day with kind words.** Whether it's an "I love you," "Have a great day," or "Sweet dreams to the gal I dream about," words are an amazing way to share your love and affection. Consider the power of your words and greetings.

2. **Thank your partner for the little things.** It's not just the big things that deserve appreciation. Think small. Does your partner unload the dishwasher? Not wake you up in the morning if you got to sleep later? Help around the house? Start saying "thank you" today at every opportunity.

3. **Tell and show your partner they are on your mind.** Find ways to show your partner consideration. Make a date. Cook a favorite dinner. Pick up your loved one's shirts from the cleaner's and save them a trip. If you are at the grocery store, call and see if they need anything special. Show you are thinking of your partner, and make life easier and more pleasant for them.

CHAPTER 4

RAISING KINDER CHILDREN

We can all raise kinder children and teach kindness, one child at a time. We give birth to kids and to kindness alike. Together we create the next generation of humankind and *humans* being *kind*. Raising kinder children is something all parents would agree is a meaningful goal. When asked what we want for our children, we often say we want our kids to be happy. What if all parents also wanted their children to be happy *and* kind? Ah, the benefits of "everyday" kind kids. I believe that happiness naturally would follow.

Kind kids are more at ease socially and learn life-long positive people-pleasing skills. All parents want their child to be kind-natured, but the moment another child is "not nice" to theirs, it can feel disheartening. The power of kindness begins at a very early age, and the benefits are staggering. Children who possess good-hearted tendencies often exhibit leadership qualities and attract more friends at an early age.

What's wonderful about kindness is that it is a skill that can be learned. As an art teacher, I taught creativity and inspired children to understand an array of materials, techniques, and aesthetic ideas that produced endless beautiful possibilities. All they had to do was add their imaginations. Teaching kids to be kind is like developing the proficiency to create a priceless work of art. Instead of being the coolest kid in the room, how about being the kindest? Raising kinder kids with a heart for helping others has a prominent place in this book. Once a child understands the importance of their actions, good deeds, and the joy of helping others, kindness becomes fun and is highly contagious.

Why Kindness Matters Most

Children have many opportunities to learn kindness from you. You are their very first teacher. Kindness is a learned response that makes the world, and *their* world, a brighter place. Parents who make considering other people's feelings a priority can attest to how these actions are modeled by their children. When you make engaging in kindness a part of your daily life, children are more likely to follow suit and truly enjoy being nice.

LOL Snapshot

A young mother shared her special family tradition that celebrated and fostered kindness at home. When her children were three and five, she started a *Family Kindness Keeper* book. Her goal was to fill it up with kindnesses that each family member (including parents) did and shared. Every day when the kids came home, they'd sit together at the kitchen table and talk about one thing they or someone else did that was nice. It could be as simple as holding open the door for another child or playing with a new classmate. No surprise, the book easily filled up! One of her children, when asked to bring in "something you are proud of," even took it to her show-and-tell at school. She beamed as she talked about her family's kind deeds.

> **LOL:** Encourage your children from a young age to try to fill your heart or someone else's with smiles. Ask what they did each day to put a smile on someone's heart. It's a special and fun way to inspire kindness. (P.S. If your child replies that "hearts can't smile," explain how no one has ever measured how much love a heart can hold, so they should keep filling it up and picture it smiling.)

Defining Kindness for Kids

Teaching a child to "care a whole lot" takes time. How we go about instilling that value is a lifelong lesson. Children practice what they are taught, both in principle and by the actions seen every day that require positive reinforcement.

Kindness starts at home. Probably every parent on the planet has said, "Be nice," "Do the right thing," "What's the magic word?" and "Nice hands, please." Start a kindness culture in your home. It's easy to do, and small acts of kindness and love shared out loud at home translate into large benefits.

When I was little, my grandmother would say, "Pretty is as pretty does." I understood that to mean that kindness is a beautiful trait. Since children understand kindness at an early age by the examples they see, beginning with their parents and other individuals around them, consider these attributes of kindness. A timely example illustrates this idea. When my grandchildren spend the night and I'm in charge of making their lunches, I add a little "I love you" note for them to discover. My granddaughter Dani reminded me to add the note last time she stayed over to ensure I wouldn't forget it. Little things mean a lot to children, and they are paying attention to everything you do or say.

Be mindful of your own actions. You are your child's best role model. Children repeat what they see and learn at home. What kind actions do you display to others daily? Are you helpful? Are you pleasant to be around? Do you look for ways to make life easier for others? Invite your children to give you a thumbs-up when you do something kind. Everyone can be in charge of kindness, if you make it a priority.

Be proud out loud. Think of ways to reinforce kindness by sharing how proud you are of the little things, words like "Kindness alert...wow, you are so sweet to help me clean up the table." Or "Here comes Mr. Mighty Manners, my superkid for thinking of others! You are so loving to make a get-well-soon card for your sister." What do you do to make it a part of your family values, family dinners, and everyday rituals? Assign your child (age two and a half to three is old enough) to be in charge of the "I love you" hugs. Our family called these "happy hugs" because we'd do a group hug, putting our daughter in the middle. When you let your kids know you're proud of them out loud just for being themselves, it goes a long way, and the hugs multiply.

Encourage an understanding of how your child affects others. Discuss how your child's actions affect other people, to build mindfulness of others and show empathy. If your child decides not to go to someone's birthday party for no valid reason, point out how this makes the birthday girl feel. Everyone's feelings matter. Or when you child is not chosen for a part in the play, teach them to recognize that it was someone else's turn, to be happy for the other person, and to keep trying. Create an awareness of how we all affect each other and can learn to celebrate others' accomplishments.

The Kinder-Word List

There are many ways to exemplify the meaning of the term *kind* to children of all ages. A fun thing to do is to create a list of kindness words (you'll be surprised how many synonyms for *kind* exist) and post it on the refrigerator, print a bookmark with the words, or put them on Post-it notes, adding hearts and ILYs ("I love you's"), in your children's lunchboxes as a reminder. Use them when praising a child, especially as they grow older!

Words to use

accommodating	good-natured	softhearted
agreeable	gracious	sweet
attentive	grateful	sympathetic
charitable	great	tender
compassionate	helpful	tenderhearted
considerate	humane	thankful
courteous	kind	thoughtful
empathetic	kindhearted	tolerant
friendly	loving	understanding
generous	neighborly	warmhearted
gentle	patient	well-meaning
giving	pleasant	willing
good	pleasing	
good-hearted	sensitive	

If your household is filled with "Hurry up — we're late" or "Stop that," create a shift by having a no-complaint, talk-nicely day. Notice your words and tone, and create a positive household one day at a time. Pick clothing out the night before a school day, get organized, and enjoy your morning. Rushing, nagging, or overdirecting can be stressful for kids and doesn't feel good for parents, either. Take the time to proactively set the tone so the day gets off to a good start for your entire family.

> **LOL:** Bring kindness to a child's level, and make it fun. Role-model niceness and watch it spread. Teach your child that when you add the *n* to *kid*, you get *kind*!

Giving Your Child a Kindness Job

Giving your kids a "kindness" mission inspires them to express their love and feelings out loud. When a child learns fun ways to make someone else smile, it's contagious. Put your child in charge of a few love songs or poems that share love. I promise, it's a gift you give yourself.

Three-year-old Sienna learned a few "I love you" songs, which she proudly sings before she goes to bed every night. She also enjoys singing the songs for family members to brighten their day. One of the irresistible tunes she learned is a classic by Nat King Cole called "L-O-V-E." She belts out her version, starting with "*L* is for the way you look at me." Talk about a little charmer! She already knows how to spread a little *L-O-V-E* everywhere she goes.

When my daughter Ali was seven years old, I taught her to make a bundt cake from a store-bought mix. It was an easy recipe for a child to make, and she mastered it very quickly. Ali's lemon cake, like the one her grandma used to make, became a popular dessert for many of our family occasions. Ali also made cakes to wish someone a "get well," express sympathy when a loved one passed, or thank a special teacher. She was quite proud of her cakes and felt such joy baking them and giving them away to brighten someone's day.

LOL Snapshot

When my son Justin was fifteen years old, he was captain of the basketball team at his high school. There was a team member who had sat on the bench the entire year and was never put into a game to play, ever. On the last day of the season, in the final three minutes of the game, the coach waved to this young man: he was in. Having given up on playing, he'd come to the last game to cheer everyone on and for the first time didn't have on his jersey. My son instantly said, "Dude, take my jersey," as he pulled it off and gave it to him. The boy jumped up, put on Justin's jersey, and played the final minutes until the buzzer rang. They won the game, and this boy felt like a million bucks. His mother called that night to share her thanks, as Justin's act of kindness was monumental in their eyes and made her son feel so special.

The face of kindness is something that is easily recognized when we see it in action, but children learn by doing and having a role. The positive effect of kindness reinforces more kindness, and over time, children discover that when you are kind, people want to play with you, invite you to come over, and be your friend. Social reward is a powerful motivator, but the core value underlying kindness is how good it feels to be nice without expecting anything in return.

How to Raise Kinder Children

Bob Burg, the coauthor of *The Go-Giver*, shared: "If I were to suggest something I've noticed that instills kindness, just from being raised by two wonderful parents, it's 'Example, example, example.' I constantly saw my parents helping others in any way they could, genuinely caring about others, and doing their best to assist them. To me that was just a part of my learned belief system. I never knew anything else."

Bob adds, "A parent can instill in their children the desire to give by simply being a person who gives. To give because it's the right thing to do. To give because they truly have a heart for helping others." As he points out, "It's not about giving back; in fact, give first! Really it's about the generous spirit of giving of oneself for no other reason than because it's congruent with one's values."

There are many things *you* can do to increase your child's kindness factor:

Be a kinder-finder. Catch your child in the act of doing something nice and say, "Your actions are so kind today. Thank you for sharing your treat with your little sister. I know she really appreciated that." When you notice even a little instance of a child using a kind voice, being thoughtful, or doing something nice for others, acknowledge it out loud. Don't go too overboard with rewards since you don't want your child to be motivated solely by the praise. But when your child does something especially noteworthy and demonstrates patience or does a wonderful deed, it's a special opportunity to notice with a high five or hug.

Build the skill. Once you've role-played, encourage your child to use their kindness powers like a superhero. Teach your kids how to ask someone to play or be their friend. Sounds simple, but it works. While superheroes save the day, encourage your child to name their kindness alter ego (such as Princess Good Heart or Captain Kinder Kid), and every time they do something superkind, you can say, "Here comes my super-kinder-hero." Praise kindness in creative ways.

Use your kinder voice. One of the first characteristics of kindness to share with kids and have them consider is tone of voice. Encourage a kind tone often. When a child uses one, say "thank you" and acknowledge it: "I love how your voice sounded so kind when you asked for an extra helping." When you answer the telephone or ask the kids to come to dinner, listen to the tone of your own voice. A kinder voice goes a long way!

Raise a helper. When children see themselves as needed and helping at home, it builds their self-esteem but also stresses the importance of giving of oneself. Children who are raised doing age-appropriate and meaningful chores gain a sense of contributing to their family and are more likely to offer to help when at school and play. Children are great at helping pick up their toys and putting away their clothes when clean, so brainstorm a list of ways your kids would like to pitch in. Helping hands are kind hands and a special family value.

Point out how kindness makes a good first impression. Kind manners and a great attitude make a wonderful impression. To reinforce your child's actions, give them your attention. Comment, "Wow, did you see your teacher's face when you asked how her day was? That was so thoughtful of you!" Children gain from understanding what it means to make a first impression. Over time, they'll see how being kind is an opportunity to make new friends.

Role-play kindness. Kids love to act things out, so put on the *Nice to Be Nice* show! My husband, Ed, built a puppet stage, which I decorated, for our grandchildren, and we filled a basket with puppets we'd find along our travels or when visiting toy stores. One of the first puppet shows four-year-old Dani put on was about a puppet who did not get along with the others. She pretended to be the teacher and encouraged the puppets to play with each other nicely. One was even put in time-out for not talking kindly to the others.

Use kinder reminders. Sometimes when a child needs a little encouragement, instead of offering it out loud, you might use a signal like a thumbs-up or two thumbs-up or a special word to remind them to be kind. If you add words to your signal, saying "thumbs-up," it means "Put your kindness hat on" or "Way to go!" It surely carries more weight than the overused phrase "Be nice!" The key is to make these kinder reminders meaningful and fun and add your very special language. The same goes for good manners, which are kind ways of responding to others.

Joey Reiman, author of *Thumbs Up!*, shared the power of thumbs-up and thinking positive: "The way to be successful in a complex world is with simple affirmations. Giving a thumbs-up is the quickest way to hope. The gesture transmits positivity."

He believes: "Thumbs-up people are positive people. When you give a child a thumbs-up, you give her affirmation. A thumbs-up carries with it a history of 'good to go,' from Roman emperors, to the astronauts, to world leaders, to moms and dads. Giving a child a thumbs-up tells him he is good to grow up. He is now a messenger who will deliver the message he has just received, creating more love in the world."

Create family volunteering projects. When each of my children was around four years old, I asked them to choose something that helped other children. My son elected to collect toys for children who didn't have any during the holidays. With the support of his school and the entire community, over twenty thousand toys were collected, and the mayor even proclaimed Justin's Miracle Makers Project a special day in Atlanta. The recognition shed light on how many underserved children would go without toys that year and how desperately they were needed for the holidays, which inspired more toys to be collected citywide. Imagine all the good it could do if every child had a kindness project at an early age!

Get involved at your child's school. When you volunteer, consider what it says to your child. It's fulfilling for you and them, and there are so many opportunities to help. Suggest to the teacher you'd like to chair the Kindness Kid-mittee. The kid-mittee (like a sunshine committee) could have kids (and their parents) doing kind deeds when a classmate is out sick, a family member is ill, another family is going through a difficult time, or someone could use cheering up. The members of the kid-mittee could all turn in suggestions to the Kindness Box when they notice a good deed that needs doing, or if they've done one, submit it to inspire the class.

Teach and instill a respect for others. Every person matters and deserves respect. Teaching children to respect each other and the environment and care for everyone and everything brightens our lives. Respect is modeled and learned, and we can all teach our children and our children's children well.

Consider consequences for unkind behavior. Let's face it. Kids misbehave and sometimes aren't so kind. For toddlers and older children who understand right and wrong, ask what they could do differently instead of pushing. What activity would your child lose if they act like that again? Be clear in your expectations, with consequences that are age appropriate, and follow through.

LOL Snapshot

A mother at one school ignited a kindness campaign with her child's kindergarten class. Another parent joined her in dressing up as Mr. and Mrs. Mighty Manners. At the first meeting with the class, they introduced themselves and had the kids brainstorm a long list of ways each child could have good manners. These little acts of kindness — ranging from offering to help the teacher tidy up, to showing a new student where to find everything in the classroom, to inviting someone to sit together at lunch, to saying "please" and "thank you" when ordering lunch — were written on slips of paper, and each child chose one. The kids were encouraged to collectively put their great big list of kind deeds and good manners into action.

It's Cool to Be Kind

There are many parent-approved initiatives online that inspire kids to be nice to each other, including teens. More than two decades ago in the kitchen of Amy Sacks Zeide's childhood home, a story on the evening news touched her deeply. Thanks to her mother's response to the then teenager, her mission of giving was born.

Here is Amy's story in her own words:

It was 1994, and I was watching the news while my mom was making dinner. I heard a story about a shelter that had been robbed the day before it was having a holiday party for their residents, and all their gifts were stolen. I was devastated. I asked my mom, "How could anyone steal from children living in a homeless shelter?"

While the story could have ended there, instead of my mom saying "Oh, isn't that sad," she replied, "What do you want to do about it?"

At that moment, I decided to use my allowance and babysitting money to buy gifts for the shelter to try to replace what had been stolen. This led to Amy's Holiday Party, which I did for many years. Building on the success of the party, I then founded Creating Connected Communities, and today our organization offers truly meaningful and direct hands-on volunteer opportunities through programs all over Atlanta. Each year we serve thousands of children and families in need and offer hundreds of teen volunteer opportunities. We create partnerships with agencies serving Atlanta families to offer community-building programs that work to create a connected community of caring and compassion.

Make Kindness Fun

Making kindness part of your daily life is a beautiful thing. So here are some enjoyable ways to express it out loud and on the go:

Notice niceness with "I spy kindness." Can your child point out other kind people doing nice things during your day? My granddaughter Bella, who is four, taught me to play her version of this popular game. Talk about these examples of people helping other people, and play I spy: "I spy with my little eye...someone helping a woman take her groceries to her car." Guess who? When your child notices other people being nice, ask them to share it with you as part of this game.

Share kind thoughts and an attitude of gratitude.
Kids love opportunities to call friends and family
members to share kind words. Practice saying "thank
you" and then try calling Grandma and share the gratitude. *Ring, ring.* "Hi, Grandma, thank you for picking
me up in car pool today. I was so happy to see you!"
Videos recorded on your smartphone are also meaningful mini-movies trumpeting your child's gratitude,
which can be followed up with a thank-you call.

Invent story starters about kindness. When driving in
the car, start a story and begin with, "Once upon a time
there was a very kind girl named Dani [your child's
name] who did nice deeds everywhere she went." Then
ask your child to add a sentence to the story, and go
back and forth. Before you know it, you'll have an entire story and be living happily and kinder ever after.

Play compliment ping-pong. This is an entertaining,
imaginative out-loud word game that goes back and
forth as you say kind compliments to each other. The
goal is to make your words sincere and loving and
make the other player feel special. You can also get very
silly and give the car or your puppy compliments —
the sky's the limit!

Surprise people with acts of kindness. Brainstorm a
list of really nice things you can do for others — for

example, leaving a small pot of flowers on someone's front doorstep or desk, maybe even anonymously. Select a month (perhaps your child's birthday month), make that your family's "Month of Kindness," and every day perform one kind act. Create a list of recipients: teachers, sisters, brothers, grandparents, friends, and service providers, including your dentist and doctor. Then refer to the list and, whenever it's possible, have your child surprise someone. The reaction will be priceless, and you and your child will smile all the way home.

Respect the earth and the environment around you. Encourage a respect for the earth. When we care, that means not littering or doing things that pollute the environment. Recycling and not being wasteful are things that children can get involved in and understand. By pitching in, volunteering to clean up our planet, and making a difference, kids learn it can be fun and rewarding to be kind. As a family we volunteered to clean up the front yard of a senior citizen who could no longer care for it herself.

Establish an "I Love You Library." An idea with longevity and purpose is to establish an I Love You Library. Beginning at your child's or grandchild's birth, fill the library with a few books for little ones. Reading to a baby, long before they are ready to comprehend it, is a wonderful habit to begin. You can read kids a goodnight book via FaceTime or telephone while you're traveling or in person when you're babysitting or at home. This time together is so special. The I Love You Library can be a drawer, shelf in a closet, or laundry basket filled with books. Include special titles like *The Giving Tree* by Shel Silverstein. Over the years, add new ones and save the books for your grandchildren's children. That collection of books will be the ones you shared and will represent time together. I love to act out some of the characters and occasionally find plush figures or puppets that go with the books. *The Very Hungry Caterpillar* or the *Sesame Street* or Dr. Seuss characters are a few favorites to share over the growing years.

Demonstrate that the sky's the limit. From the sun coming up to the sun setting to twinkling stars in the sky, seize the moment and teach your kids about the galaxy. Name a star for each child. The North Star could be your oldest and so on. Look for the Big Dipper and the Little Dipper. Teach your kids about the stars, and enjoy not only an educational lesson but a "far-out" way to have fun and share positive thoughts of what it means to shine bright, lighting up other people's lives like the stars light up the sky! We all remember looking at clouds and seeing creatures and all kinds of imaginary figures in the clouds. This tried-and-true activity is a wonderful way to keep your kids entertained.

Bestow paper-plate awards. Turn ordinary paper plates into actual Superkid awards. Think about ways you can inspire your children to feel good about themselves, whether they cleaned up your guest room or were nice to their baby sister. From World's Nicest Kid to "I kept my hands to myself," the awards can vary depending on what you want to teach your kids. If you're an aunt, uncle, grandparent, or teacher, have the kids take the awards home to build self-esteem.

Initiate the Better Letter. When you have a babysitter over, leave a piece of paper and an envelope on the table. Invite the babysitter to write what your children did better each time — something kind, good-natured, or helpful — and put it in the envelope and seal it up. The next day, open the envelope and read aloud what your children did that was better and showed progress. Give your kids a big hug, keep these compliments in a special place, and remind them next time the babysitter comes back what they did to earn kind words.

Celebrate kindness. Kids love parties, and a kinder-party is a fun activity for them to organize. Kids can bake cookies, put on some music, invite a few friends, and celebrate someone who needs cheering up or has been ultra-kind. Throw a t-party (*t* is for "thankful") in honor of a child or other family member who has gotten well, your dog or cat who is back home after a stay at the vet's, or a nice neighbor you want to invite over and thank for bringing in your mail. Consider how to turn a kinder-party into a wonderful opportunity to focus on someone who is deserving and profess appreciation. Each child gets a turn thanking the guest of honor.

How to Avoid Overindulging Kids

Overindulging kids is one of the things we as parents and grandparents do all too often. Bombarded with the latest toys, crazes, and trends, we can find it easy to buy into the instant gratification, knowing we'll put a huge smile on our kids' and grandkids' faces. However, we all know that most toys lose their luster. And even worse, when they receive a lot of gifts at once, kids don't even remember who gave them what.

Sometimes it's the little things that help children be grateful for and appreciate a gift. When giving a gift, include coupons you make yourself for playing time or book reading. Or, instead of running out and buying toys every time you see your grandchildren, try this idea. I occasionally add new board games to our toy closet to reinforce reading and counting skills. These items remain at our house for all our grandchildren to look forward to, enjoy, and reuse. It's also so much fun to play together and share.

Another clever idea is inspired by our five-year-old grandson, who challenged us to a game of his version of Trivial Pursuit. He made up all the questions (from "How many legs are on an insect?" to "What's my favorite candy?"). We had a blast playing his technology-free, good old-fashioned pencil-and-paper question-asking game he designed all by himself, and we learned wonderful things about him and his special interests.

Another idea for giving a lasting gift is to find out what lessons a child is interested in taking and consider teaching or funding this new skill or hobby. Focus on a gift that builds a talent — learning to play the game of chess, for example, or a musical instrument — and offers lifelong joy.

Encourage Spreading Kindness

Throughout a child's life, there are endless opportunities to inspire them to kindness! From celebrating a child's birthday with a kindhearted twist to volunteering, kids love helping their parents make a difference. Here are some suggestions that take the emphasis off "me" and include the idea of "we." How can *we* make a difference? Who can *we* help?

Bookbag buddies. Be nice. Think twice. At the beginning of every school year, one family instilled a special way to give, as each child filled their own backpack with supplies for the new school year, they also filled a backpack for another child the same age and donated the bookbags to a good cause.

A giving-back birthday party. Brainstorm with your child how to make each birthday include a "giving back" theme, donating and doing something special for someone else. For example, one seven-year-old had the idea to ask his friends to bring a new or gently used book to his birthday party. He decorated a bin to collect the books and then donated them to a lending library at a homeless shelter, which was ecstatic to receive his birthday books every year. For each birthday, another family encourages their children to do as many good deeds as their actual age. (In other words, turning five would be five kind deeds in honor of the birthday.) It's fun to count (the years) by kindness.

The birthday rule. Before your child's next birthday, make it a meaningful yearly habit to clean out the old toys they have outgrown or no longer play with and donate them to a good cause that appreciates used toys in great condition. Involving your kids is key. Together clean them up, pack up the pieces, and select where they go, perhaps to a nearby nonprofit or shelter. Volunteer your time at this cause and get involved. The goal is not to clean up the closet and allow for more, but to instill an awareness of others year-round and give your time, not just the toys.

The "one toy" rule. When kids have too many toys or are indulged with material objects, they can become overwhelmed with all the choices and only gravitate to the new ones. An idea we implemented at our house and to this day I still enforce is the "one-toy-closet" rule. After playing with a toy from the closet, you must put it back before taking out another one. This avoids having a room filled with so many toys that kids don't have a respect for them. It also helps you stay organized, without a sea of toys and a great big mess.

Grateful giving on Thanksgiving. During the month of November in the lead-up to Thanksgiving, involve your kids in making signs and flyers for a neighborhood can-donation collection effort and in helping to gather approved food choices with a long shelf life for a local food-drive campaign. An awareness of those who are hungry whom we can all help is important to teach a child.

Bundles for babies. Many homeless shelters are in need of basic items, like diapers. One family collected diapers from other families and delivered them monthly to an area shelter. The diaper drive became a citywide effort, and many communities and nonprofits were appreciative to receive these bundles for the babies and toddlers who needed them.

The umbrella campaign. My friend Ava and her then five-year-old, Meredith, used to purchase inexpensive umbrellas and keep a dozen of them on board. They would give them out whenever it rained. There would always be someone caught without one and in need. Another mom and her kids filled bookbags with personal-care items and distributed them to neighbors following a destructive flood.

Thank-you-note fun. We have a small desk filled with thank-you stationery and stickers at home in the kids' playroom. On occasions when there's a reason our grandchildren have stayed overnight, the desk is ready in case they want to write a thank-you note for all the fun we had. It's another art project they love doing, but also a meaningful way to make thank-you-note writing fun and role-model kindness.

Turn the prom into a promise. To add purpose to the prom, one teen honored fallen soldiers by writing their names on ribbons on her prom dress, which she designed. Another prom-goer forewent the expensive dinner and pledged to donate the money to a pet-adoption shelter he volunteered at monthly.

Welcoming a Baby Out Loud with Love

Kindness starts early, and so does loving a child out loud. Children are more likely to believe words they hear praising something specific. Tell them you love them every day. From nursery rhymes to songs, there are countless ways to make a child feel loved. Give a child a loving nickname, your time, and unconditional attention. Read to them often, as a love of learning begins at home.

Here are some little "I love you" phrases that show love and will go over big:

- Ask "How much do I love you?" and encourage a back-and-forth display of how far your love goes.

Make it fun for a child to answer with creative ideas like "To the moon and back." Or "To planet Mars and back" or "To the north pole and back!" Give it a try!

- Whenever you are with your child or grandchild, ask the LOL question "What's my favorite time of the day?" Smile and answer, "Right now with you!" Before you know it, when you ask your child "What's my favorite time of day?" they will answer with you in unison.

- When a child says "I love you," reply "I love you more!" or "I love you most!" Think of creative ways to respond. "I love you to infinity and beyond!"

- Play an "I love you" counting game. Begin with "I love you ONE," then the child replies with "I love you TWO," after which you add "I love you THREE," and the game continues as high as your child can count.

- Think of a special nickname to call a child:

  o "Hello, my love bug."
  o "Good night, my little petunia."
  o "You are my funny bunny."

Try to create your own songs and "I love you" sayings! When my son was born, I wrote a song and accompanying music. Go for it! Love your children and grandchildren out loud. Your words will be enjoyed for a long, long time!

Here are some additional suggestions that will help

you prepare to love a child out loud in a truly meaningful way:

Ready, set, read! It's never too early to read to a child. A wonderful book to read out loud even to a new baby is *I Already Know I Love You*. Billy Crystal, the famous actor and comedian, wrote this touching book about loving a grandchild before the child is born. Give this book to your expecting children, along with a tape of you reading the first few pages out loud. Inscribe the book to your future grandchild, personalizing it if you know your selected name, and if not, just sign it from "Grandma and Grandpa" or "Someone who thinks you're 'grand' and loves you — a lot!" Leave a message on an expecting parent's cell phone saying, "Hi, my precious grandbaby on your way, I already know I love you!" Also, check out Hoda Kotb's books *I've Loved You Since Forever* and *You Are My Happy*, which will warm your heart and share your love out loud, including in families with adopted children.

Write now — talk it up later! When Dani, our precious granddaughter, was on the way, I began writing a letter in a pretty blank book every time I felt I had something to impart to her to welcome her into the world. I reflected on when her daddy was a baby and shared how much fun we'd have when she arrived. Since that day, I have taken the time to add a letter to the book each year and tape keepsakes like her birthday invitations or photographs in it. I named the book *Dear Dani*, and what makes the book so special is that now that she is six years old, I read her pages from it and still write in it often. Family members, certainly grandparents, will enjoy your *Dear Baby* book. Start it even before a child is born.

LOL Snapshot

[Example]

Dear Dani:

Ever since I heard you were coming into our lives, I was already in love. I knew that you'd be the most beautiful addition to our family. Your mommy and daddy have been busy lovingly preparing for your welcome to this world. Now that you have arrived and are just a day old, there are a few things about me I want you to know. I promise to be there when you need me. I am a call away. I promise to clap the loudest at your performances. I am a call away. I promise to make you the best cookies you've ever tasted and teach you how to bake. I am a call away. I promise to love you to the moon and back. I am a call away. You are my sunshine, the light of our lives, and we will forever love you with all of our hearts. I am a call away!

With all my love and the biggest welcome with forever hugs,

Grandma Ro Ro

Love children across the miles. For grandparents or family members who live in other cities or a parent who travels often, it sometimes might seem hard to connect. But whenever you are apart, fear not! Your daily calls and FaceTime check-ins will make all the difference. Another idea involves sending postcards back and forth. Kids love to get mail, and it's especially exciting to get a letter or postcard in this electronic age. Pre-stamp a selection of postcards addressed to you, give them as a gift, and encourage your grandchild to send you postcard drawings to proudly display on your refrigerator or wall. The next time they visit, they'll love seeing the gallery of their postcard art.

Keep in mind as you raise kinder children, it's an on-going opportunity to encourage collective kindness. I love how my daughter-in-law Jaime urges my grandchildren to *lead with kindness*. A former kindergarten teacher, she observed over the years that this motto was something even young children understand, and it works.

LOL Snapshot

A faraway grandparent shared, "Every day at five, rain or shine, if it was at all possible, my husband and I made sure to call our daughter and then granddaughter and grand-son when they were old enough to receive the calls. Our telephone or FaceTime call daily was a special hello. The consistency of that daily call gave them and us something to look forward to. From reading a book (chapter books once they got older) to showing them cookies I baked for a friend who was sick, we found even five minutes of FaceTiming to be a wonderful way to include them and spend quality time. We started sharing all the kind things we do for others, and we'd be so proud of even the littlest good deed on their part. Imagine that, five hundred miles away. We all look forward to these togetherness calls!"

> **LOL:** Together, we can teach kids that kindness really counts. To be kind, you don't have to be the fastest runner, the smartest student, the most musically inclined band member, a gifted artist, or the best at anything. Everyone has the same hours in the day to be nice and friendly, and we all have the superpower to be superkind.

Three LOL Things You Can Do Today to Raise Kind Kids

1. **Role-model kindness at home.** Think of how you speak to your children and family. Kids will model what they see and hear. Be the kindest role model you can be, and teach your children kindness at a very young age.

2. **View kindness as being helpful.** Kindness is being nice, but it's also defined as helping others. Talk with your children about how they can give someone a hand and make a difference. Kids can be helpful in endless ways. Give a big hand for your kids' helping hands.

3. **Celebrate kindness now.** When you see someone being kind, thank them. When your children are thoughtful and caring and demonstrate kind behaviors, give them a thumbs-up, a high five, or a big hug.

CHAPTER 5

LOVING YOUR FRIENDS OUT LOUD

Through the years, friends come in and out of our lives. Friends lift us up, share our joys and sorrows, and sustain us. If you have close lifelong friends, you are one of the lucky ones. What a gift! True friends show endless care and share words that soothe, motivate, calm, inspire, and support each other. Learning how to love each of our friends out loud takes time, and it helps to understand the uniqueness of each friendship.

This chapter embraces the importance of our relationships with our friends. As we build friendships, it's vital to accept others, along with their shortcomings. That does not mean removing your boundaries or befriending just anyone, but it does mean celebrating your friends, acknowledging their strengths and accepting their weaknesses.

A loving and warm friendship can be one of life's most beautiful gifts. Friendship is what happens naturally when two people care about each other's well-being and feel connected. To have friends, we must *be* a friend and become the type of friend we want for ourselves. It begins with being a friend to yourself. Open yourself up and be aware of how you affect others, and make your friendships a priority. Our treasures in life are friends, who also can become like family.

A Friend Is a Gift You Give Yourself

What kind of friend are you? Good, better, or best? If you have a friend who's truly there for you, you're fortunate. It's a two-way street, and feeling supported and heard is important. How you treat your friends and respond to their needs contributes to the quality of the ones you keep. The key to friendship is spending time together, sharing each other's lives, and staying in touch.

To be a "love out loud" friend, consider these things:

Do you truly know and understand your friends? Ask yourself if you are aware of what it's like to be in your friends' shoes. Are you sensitive to your friends' time constraints and schedules? Do you know what's going on in their lives? Knowing your friends inside and out takes time, mutual respect, and an investment of energy and understanding.

Conversely, friends who "get" you realize you work and have nonstop family responsibilities and other obligations, and they understand if you are missing in action. They check in on you. They know what you value and also value you. They do not judge you, and they offer to help: from driving car pool to giving you a shoulder to lean on in tough times. They are constant companions, celebrating your happiness and offering support during loss or hardship.

Are you a reciprocal friend? We all need different types of friends who bring out the best in us, as we do them. A great friendship is reciprocal in many ways. You make time for your friends. You brighten their lives; they brighten yours. Be it with a regular lunch date, a walk in the park, or meaningful conversations by phone, good friends show concern for each other and are inclusive. You introduce one circle of friends to another and put all on the guest list. Close friends don't just wait for invitations; they understand the gift of reciprocity and also proactively invite everyone to get together.

Are you supportive of your friends during life's transitions? Friends support, celebrate with, and console each other during some of life's most important transitions (from marriage to having a baby to the death of a loved one). Friends offer us encouragement and understanding and lift us up in so many ways, especially through the most difficult times. Are you there for your friends in happy and sad times alike? Are you *still* there days, weeks, and months later? Do you give support, space, and room to grow to your friends who are not at their best while experiencing challenges? The ebb and flow of friendship involves giving and receiving. Friends are nonstop supportive and show up 24-7 when needed if it's possible.

Who is your everything? If you feel very close to a friend, it's always special to tell them so. Recently when I introduced my friend Lisa to a group of my friends, without delay she announced to all of them, "Robyn is my everything." At first, I was speechless; it was the ultimate compliment and display of friendship. Lisa and I have been friends for over fifty years, and that touched me deeply. Her kind words made me feel so appreciated and loved. I often echo her words in my mind and am so grateful to be a treasured friend of Lisa's, just as she will always be one of mine as well. True friends are etched in each other's hearts.

> **LOL:** Friends make your world a kinder place. Treasure your friends and do not take friends for granted. Ever.

How to Be an "Attagirl" or "Attaboy" Friend

Friends who cheer us on in life step in during the most mundane of times, not just the happy ones. They share our joy but also lift us up when we're down and know how to lighten our loads when things in life seem insurmountable.

Are You a Go-to Friend?

I have friends I call for fashion advice, relationship insights, nutritional guidance, exercise motivation, life inspiration, and more. Be somebody's go-to friend and share your time and talents.

Edie Fraser is one of my treasured go-to friends. She is the founder of STEMconnector, a collaborative to build science, technology, engineering, and mathematics (STEM) talent; Million Women Mentors (MWM), the largest mentor-matching initiative, with 2.3 million commitments between girls and women from middle school upward; and Diversity Best Practices. She is also the winner of fifty-four awards celebrating women, diversity, and leadership. Edie is very vocal about "doing your giving while you are living." From the moment we met over two decades ago, we became fast friends, and at every turn Edie, with her effervescent, generous personality, shares her "attagirl" mentoring with everyone she meets. The gratitude she offers spans the miles due to her frequent check-in and thank-you calls to a multitude of friends, and she encourages each of us by sharing such kindhearted "you can do it" feelings.

Another story illustrates the importance of not delaying expressing your gratitude to friends. Howard Miller, a retired physician, shared a most poignant view of friendship:

> I lost a dear friend, who was also my patient, to cancer. He reinforced for me the value of the people closest to you. You can move along on autopilot, as we all do, and never quite take the time to think about the valuable contribution of close friends and family to the quality of your life. Sharing thoughts and just simple day-to-day events with them makes life fuller and more. It's been four years, and I'm still reliving this loss. I wish he was with us, and daily, I think about things we shared, what we cared about, and how much I still want to share with him. This has overflowed into the rest of my relationships, and it amplified my thoughts about treasuring the people who make life whole.

Dr. Miller concluded:

> Being a physician and dealing with life-and-death matters in a real way, you block out some level of emotional response to certain

events to get through life. You are still caring and compassionate, but there has to be some separation, or you would never get through the days. People in your close circle, however, transcend all of that, and it is vitally important to remember how much they mean to you and embrace the moment.

> **LOL:** Be the type of friend you wish to have, and stay connected. Think of what type of friend you value most and what kind you'd like to be considered as well. Every day do one thing that brings your own friendship qualities to life, whether it's being generous, kindhearted, thoughtful, or fun and upbeat.

Listening to Your Friends

While this book is about loving others out loud, one of the most important qualities expressing love is *listening*. If you're a good friend, you can repeat the sequence of events or details of a story another friend is sharing. In other words, you're an expert listener. You hear what's going on in your friend's life that day and what's on their mind at that moment. Timing is everything.

Don't interrupt or turn the conversation to yourself at every turn: "Oh, I've been to that city," or "That happened to me, too," or even "I know exactly what you mean; when I was younger, I had the same experience...blah, blah, blah." While having things in common brings friends closer, and is acceptable in moderation, it's also meaningful not to insert yourself at every opportunity.

As an active listener, you confirm with eye contact and body language that you are being attentive to the conversation. The signals and affirmative comments you give to the speaker let your friend know that you are interested and care about the conversation. While close friends hold each other's feelings in total confidence, they aren't secretive, nor do they cause you to walk on eggshells when you are around them. They make you feel secure, as you do the same to them, and there is a sacred trust between you.

To determine if you are a good listener, ask yourself these questions:

- Do you hear and recall everything your friend says? After a phone conversation, consider what was important about the call that you can follow up on or respond to with concern later. If you are quick to forget, then jot down a reminder to yourself. It's difficult to keep up with each other's travel schedules and other activities. Listen for dates that are worthy of remembering and take note.

- Do you give your friend your undivided attention? Friends (and everyone else, for that matter) know when you are not listening. If they seem distracted themselves, rather than unkindly commenting,

"You're not listening," simply ask your friend if this is a good time to talk.

- Are you multitasking when you talk or truly listening? Again, giving your attention to a friend validates that their thoughts are important to you. When you listen with your heart, a friend knows and feels it.

Things you can do to be a good listener and supporter

- Respond with a comment that shows you heard what your friend said: "You really had a hard day today, and I'm here for you," or "I love listening to your new outlook on life and am so proud of you for thinking positive."
- Ask a question: "Can I help you in any way to feel better?" Call your friend back within a reasonable amount of time, and if they shared something important, follow up to see how things are going.
- Show compassion: "I really care that you had a difficult experience, and perhaps I could go with you next time to make it easier" or "This, too, shall pass. Remember, tomorrow is a brand-new day."
- Focus on your friend: "I really want to hear how you are doing. Is this a good time for you to talk?" When your friend has something important happening, offer your support by calling and showing sincere interest. Give your friend a "I'm so happy for you" turn: "Tell me what was wonderful about your day today."

Share the "News at 11" with Your Friends

Want to stay in touch with friends? Communicate your intention and be consistent. Tell your friend, "I really want to hear how you are doing." My friend Linda calls it "news at 11," and when I in turn ask what she's been up to, she replies, "Five-foot-eight." All kidding aside, she is a remarkable friend who is always interested in others, and when she asks how things are going, she *listens.* Whenever Linda and I talk about the "news at 11," I know she's happy to hear from me, and it's now our special language, as we both enjoy catching up on each other's days and lives.

Remember, practice makes patience. Whatever we work at, we are more likely to become. When we practice listening, we also are practicing patience. Listening requires cultivating the ability to focus in order to truly hear someone. When we give others our undivided attention, we communicate the message that they are important to us.

> **LOL:** Today make it a point to be a good listener. Give it a try during each conversation, and afterward reflect on how you think you did. Go for the gold! Listen with your mind and heart, in addition to your ears. Be happy for your friends, sincerely interested in their lives, and compassionate when they need a shoulder to lean or cry on.

Ask Yourself, "Who Needs Me Today?"

In order to practice loving out loud, every day I think about *Who needs me today?* Four words and a simple question that keep me on track.

When I get in touch with those friends in my life who would appreciate a call, a few kind words, my attention, or support, it keeps me connected to what really matters in life and my core values of kindness and caring. While not every friend needs you around the clock, it's special when you check in and help a friend solve a problem, face a situation with confidence, or ease a little — or big — life challenge. You also need to make time to share laughter and fun with friends, so don't forget "happy talk." Call a friend to chat about how proud you are of their achievements or to get excited for them during good times. Invite them to share the details of a recent trip, a special family occasion, or something important. Notice even small steps of improvement by a friend who has gotten through a difficult illness, and cheer them on. Stay connected.

Television personality and talk-show host Christine Pullara shared how she does it:

> When it comes to my friends, lately we are all so busy, so a call or even a text checking in with my friends always brightens my day. I also make it a point to carve out time for my friends as often as I can. I didn't get married

until I was thirty-seven, so my friends were my family and my life. Lunches, shopping dates, movie nights…these are a must for me to feel connected to them and their lives. I had a friend who was going through a tough time, and she felt abandoned by some people. Recently, she let me know how much she appreciated my loyalty during that time. That's what true friends are for.

> **LOL:** Be a loyal friend. Don't forget about your friends who are struggling in life and need you. Even if you don't know what to say, check in. A phone message, at the very least, can still convey your concern and be comforting to a friend in need. When in doubt about how to approach them, ask your friend if they prefer text, email, or a call. Embrace the tough times, even when it's uncomfortable for you.

Making New Friends and Volunteering

Being *friendly* is the path to making friends. We all know gregarious people who seem to be able to effortlessly talk to new people, are open to making new friends, and value each person they encounter, including strangers. In fact, they know no strangers. Within minutes they can find out if someone loves to walk, play golf, or cook; solicit a favorite restaurant recommendation; and even make a tennis date.

Being interested in others' interests will help you

discover what you and someone new have in common. When you look a new acquaintance in the eyes, say a sincere hello and make a concerted effort to connect. While you might be shy, think of an easy question that you can answer in turn as well. *Which book are you reading? What movies have you seen lately?* It's an opportunity to open yourself up to the possibility of a new friend.

Some of my most treasured friendships have been discovered while volunteering for a worthy cause. While I have friends whom I love to shop, eat out, and even do absolutely nothing with, one of my favorite things to do with friends is volunteer. Volunteering has so many benefits. You broaden your circle of friends and meet so many new people while making a difference. It's one of the most meaningful ways to spend time together, either supporting your friends' passions for giving back or discovering your own.

When a friend or family member cares about a cause or mission, ask how you can assist. When I've asked friends to join my efforts to raise money for a cause I truly care about, I am touched when they say yes and get involved. I respect those who aren't up to the task for whatever reason, but it's a joy to share volunteerism, and caring is contagious. Before you turn down an opportunity to volunteer, learn about your friend's cause and why it means so much to them. Perhaps you can help in other ways, if volunteering is not for you, and show up at their benefit performance or inquire how things are going.

When you care about what your friends care about, you demonstrate kindness and are a thoughtful friend indeed. Donating your time, talents, or treasures to causes that are important to each other keeps you connected. Your gift of giving keeps on giving.

LOL Snapshot

My friend Nancy, always looking for ways to help others by showing up and offering a hand, volunteered with her daughter Jenny to help me, Bettye (whom I profiled in chapter 1), and her family feed the hungry. Together we served a home-cooked meal to 180 homeless individuals in Atlanta living under a bridge in the freezing cold. I was so inspired by Nancy's good deed that I made sure I volunteered for another friend's cause that following week to keep the giving going. I also learned more about what was important to Nancy and truly appreciated her good heart along with her daughter's.

> **LOL:** Brighten your life and the lives of others by volunteering for a cause. You'll discover new friends, a deeper purpose, and share time with others while making a difference.

Ways to be an LOL friend

- **Alert your friends!** Keep your friends up to date or notified about something helpful, be it a cause, a meaningful event, food, fun, a friend's birthday, or a newsy update. See something on sale or a special item you know your friend's grandchildren will love, put it on hold, text them a photo, and call up with your friend-alert sighting.

- **Notice the blues.** Consider who might be under the weather, lonely, going through a hard time, or dealing with a medical challenge, and call them up. Instead of rattling off all about your day, inquire how theirs was and listen with love. Leave a mailbox, doorman, or doorstep surprise of a card, note, treat, or gift that might offer a little TLC and comfort.

- **Laugh out loud.** Sharing a good laugh with a friend is the best. Re-create a memory from the past that was funny. Bring photographs of your past hairstyles and school pictures. When my childhood friend took me out for a birthday lunch, I brought my autograph book from camp when we were ten years old, school yearbooks, and letters saved from friends decades ago. We had a good laugh, and it was priceless.

- **Put yourself in your friend's shoes.** Think through what a friend is really going through and, while you might not have an inkling of what their situation feels like, try to understand their point of view. If a friend is having a hard time, working nonstop, or not feeling well, consider ways you can lift their spirits. Staying in touch and finding out how you can help are among the most significant bond builders. Offer to drop off homemade soup, take the kids to dinner and a movie, or run an errand. Or don't ask for permission to do a nice deed — just do it. Send a list of uplifting movies or shows you and other friends have loved to help her pass the time. Leave a basket filled with flowers or fresh fruit at their door, or coordinate a food train providing meals of their choice. One devoted family member showed up early on the day of a funeral and planted their front door planters, which were withering, in memory of her cousin's father who had passed.

- **Respond to your friends' kind deeds or actions.** Evie, an extremely gifted writer, penned me a thank-you for the vintage dresser jar filled with sixty-five shiny pennies I gave her on her sixty-fifth birthday. She wrote, "Your deep goodness and caring ways are without equal." I could almost hear Evie saying this, and her note touched me deeply. Think of who has done something for you without equal.

- **Create LOL nicknames.** My mother Phyllis's nickname was Nikki, and her best friend in college, Joan, was Juana. I grew up knowing how much my mother loved Joan and all her closest friends because of their affectionate nicknames. My friend Patty's nickname is Pisha, and her college roommate Ava's is Aviva. Patty calls hearing her nickname a love tap that makes her feel special. Sally earned the nickname Sunshine from her group of friends because she brightened everyone's day. For whatever reason, nicknames are a secret language of friends, and these loving monikers live on for decades.

• **Observe your friends' likes and dislikes.** True friends pay attention and are in tune to each other and what they need. Norma does not like tomatoes. Patty has an aversion to cumin. Freddy and Warren are gluten-free. If someone is allergic to perfume or particular foods, afraid of heights, or even diabetic, great friends are in sync with and anticipate their needs.

Keeping in Mind That Hurt Happens

Friends remember what you say and how you make them feel, and misunderstandings are potentially inevitable even among the best of friends. When a friend does something that hurts your feelings, be it an unkind remark or even leaving you out of a group activity, give it some thought before getting upset, and think through your words before responding. What do you really want to accomplish by discussing it?

For some, telling the friend in a kind way how this made you feel is imperative. For others, it's best to opt to let things roll off your back. Lindsey couldn't go to sleep unless she told her BFF, Carole, when she did something that upset her. Carole harbored her feelings and preferred not to address it at all. Everything on earth that any friend does seems to upset Lindsey. Each friendship is different and unique, and there is no one-stop shop for conflict resolution or a single way to communicate with friends. When you feel uneasy, ask yourself what you want to accomplish by talking, and envision the outcome you wish to achieve. Work toward better understanding your own feelings and actions.

Maxine Rosen, an Atlanta psychotherapist who specializes in relationships, advised: "When you share your feelings with a friend, especially with respect to a conflict or topic that is bothering you, it's important to be aware of how the other person will hear you. Understanding the consequences of what you say and how the other person perceives you is key. Think about the outcome of your words, and be aware of *What does that person hear me saying?*"

If you have a falling-out with someone and wish to repair the relationship, apologize, or even forgive the other person, make an effort to do so out loud and in person. If you elect to write a letter forgiving someone or asking for forgiveness, follow it up with a call. Keep in mind there are two sides to every story. You can agree to disagree, if the friendship matters, but if you ever want it to be stronger, consider a thoughtful way to remedy the situation. That sometimes means being kind in lieu of being right.

Maxine added:

Most of us are a little hesitant when making friends, and if someone does not pay us attention, our feelings get hurt too fast and expectations are too high. As I grow older, I realize I still must work with my newer relationships. I need to call these friends. If you have a knot in your gut when you are with someone, you can avoid them or, if it has roots and meaning, confront it and address it kindly. I don't believe in divorcing a friend, but there are friends whose moral values you can wean yourself away from, and you don't have to be in a situation that is uncomfortable. When it comes to friends, and all relationships, you have to pick what's really important and let go of the inconsequential things that don't really matter.

A few conversation starters when you've grown apart or there has been a falling-out include:

- "We haven't talked in a while — how are you doing?"
- "You've been on my mind a great deal, and I was wondering how things are going in your life."
- "I've missed talking to you. Do you have time to talk, as I was wondering if you are upset with me for any reason?"
- "I am feeling a little sensitive these days and just

wanted to know if there's anything on your mind that's bothering you."

- "It appears we might have different views of how we see a situation. Could we get together and talk about it in person? I value your friendship and would appreciate that opportunity."

- "We haven't seen each other much lately, and I'd love to know if you are up for getting together to catch up."

> **LOL:** Friendship goes both ways and takes time and attention to build, both in good and bad times. Focus on what's right with your friendship, not just what's wrong. You'll discover more of what's right.

Celebrating Friends and Establishing Traditions

Sharing time together is a love-out-loud experience. By creating a tradition that brings a group of friends together, you are more likely to maintain close contact and look forward to celebrating each other, whether it be a special occasion or no occasion at all.

Having friendship rituals builds relationships. Over the years I have found that rituals set up opportunities to get together. Since we're all so busy in life, these little traditions inspire and motivate us to hold tight to our friends and connect by spending time together. Here are a few ideas:

- Recognize special occasions, especially big birthdays and anniversaries.

- Designate a specific time to get together in person with walking or coffee dates.
- Check in on friends regularly to see how they are doing with a catch-up call.
- Be generous with your time and attention when it comes to your friends who need you.
- Consider ways to support a friend who has hit a rough patch, and mobilize a group of friends to help.
- When a friend is hosting a special event or occasion, offer to arrive early to help set up, or even help take photographs. Be specific with your offers, and avoid just asking if there's anything you can do, which is generic.
- Include your friends in your life with other friends and your family. Friendships are meant to be shared.

There are many occasions that make up a year. Share and celebrate out loud with friends those momentous moments, from birthdays to anniversaries to engagements to the birth of a child. Being happy for a friend doubles their joy and yours.

Here are some ideas for acknowledging or celebrating friends:

Have a "grateful for girlfriends" party. One year a friend gave the ideal luncheon, with a grateful-for-girlfriends theme. She had lost her mother the previous year and just really wanted to thank everyone for being so thoughtful and caring. She toasted each friend at the party with a sentiment expressing out-loud gratitude.

Honor the birthday girls. For the past thirty years (and counting), a group of my close friends celebrates each person's birthday at a dinner or lunch together. We chip in and take turns doing the planning. On the big-decade birthdays, we contribute a set amount and also give a gift, and half of that on half birthdays. This consistent get-together continues to be a way we are reunited as friends through the good and not-so-good times. We also celebrate engagements and give each newly engaged daughter or daughter-in-law-to-be a shower and a special monogrammed vase with her new initials.

Have a pancake breakfast. If you "flat-out" adore a friend or group of friends, have a pancake-breakfast tradition or a themed meal to share your affection and gratitude, and stack it up with love and pour on the syrup. Or have an omelet party for a few "good eggs" you appreciate.

Mix up your friends! Introducing your old friends to new ones you think they would like is a meaningful act of inclusiveness. I love bringing different groups of friends together, be it at a dinner party or for a casual lunch. My closest friends have become close friends, and that is a special thing. Good friends appreciate and will thank you for broadening their circle of friends as well. One year I assembled my friends who all have a September birthday and did a luncheon in their honor. Many of them did not know each other, and the synergy was wonderful.

Mark the occasion. All our friends have occasions in their lives that are momentous. Just recently our dear friend got engaged, and at every turn, we found ways to recognize their newfound relationship. At a restaurant we asked the chef to personalize a dessert for the couple and snapped a photo. It was a picture-perfect moment and made them feel very special. Moments like these give all of us joy as we celebrate our close friends' happiness.

Gift "a penny for your thoughts." For my friend's fifty-fifth birthday, I went to the bank and secured fifty-five shiny, brand-new pennies. The teller was very kind to facilitate my request, as she had to do this one penny at a time. I put them in a small satin bag and placed it inside a Victorian dresser jar that had her initials. The gift was a priceless hit!

Join the boys' club. This idea works for women and men alike. My husband goes out to dinner every month with two of his guy friends. They take turns each time and surprise the other two with a new restaurant. They've done this for over fifteen years and never repeated a restaurant. At each meal they catch up on each other's lives and critique the meal. Occasionally they later end up bringing the wives there when a restaurant is a hit. It's a wonderful tradition that has kept them close throughout the years.

Enjoy fun and games with the Wednesday Girls. My mother played mah-jongg with her "Wednesday Girls" for over sixty years. Every week they put a little cash in the kitty, and when the amount added up, they'd take a trip or do something fun together. Her Wednesday Girls were a special part of her life, and this tradition helped them remain friends for decades. When my mother passed, I saved her mah-jongg set and the quarters used in her last game in a wallet. It's one of the memories I treasure.

Be a family of friends. Christine, mother of two daughters, shared, "I'm so blessed that my daughters are best friends. They bicker a bit (who doesn't?), but they know our motto: *family first!* We do lots of girly things together, like shopping and manicures. It's so much fun to have these little ladies in my life. I hope and pray they will continue to love and support each other their entire lives."

Have a happy Friendsgiving. Recently I heard about a group of women who continue a special tradition. As Thanksgiving approaches, each girlfriend bakes a dozen servings of her all-time best dessert. They then get together and exchange goodies so that everyone leaves with a dozen "special somethings" baked by friends. They also started a Friendsgiving cookbook with copies of their cherished recipes for each of the delicacies. At their celebration, they share what they are grateful for and celebrate the friend group.

Have a standing date. If there's a flea or antique market that comes to your area monthly, have a standing date with a friend who shares your interest in vintage items and collectibles. It's fun to look forward to that get-together. My mom, who was my dedicated, beloved best friend, and I went to the same Scott Antiques Market show for over thirty years, and it was a very special time reserved for us. To this day, my husband and I continue the tradition.

Check this out! Whenever Marcia finds a fabulous audiobook at the library, she recommends it to me. I've loved her choices, including Oprah Winfrey's *What I Know for Sure*, and enjoyed listening to every word during my travels. Some days I didn't even want to get out of the car while Oprah was sharing her stories in her own inspiring voice, as I felt like she was talking to me. Marcia is so thoughtful!

Treasure your childhood friends. Friends from your childhood are often cemented in your life through cherished moments in time. One of my elementary-school friends recently planned the fiftieth reunion of her sweet-sixteen party, getting everyone who had been there together. Another planned to call everyone in her first-grade class photo. Childhood friends will always be precious. Contact yours today! Revisiting your childhood friends, no matter your age, is a gift you give yourself.

Treasure your ditch friends. A friend of mine shared, "Ditch friends are the kind of friends you could call to pull you out of a ditch." Some people call these forever friends; others call them besties or BFFs. You know who I'm talking about. Being honored as someone's closest friend is a tribute meant to last for life.

> **LOL:** Forever friends are priceless. To maintain and grow the friendship into a beautiful lasting treasure, invest time and kindness, and share your lives as friends. Honor people who are your everything. Tell them so. Thank each friend in a million little ways. Celebrate your friends by loving them out loud over time.

Three LOL Things You Can Do Today to Build Friendships

1. **Show appreciation for your friends.** There are many ways to do so, including spending time together and checking in. Give your friends your time and talents. Help a friend find shoes that fit,

look for a dress for a special occasion, or organize a closet or kitchen, and check up on them to see if they need you. Share your skills and lend a friend a hand.

2. **Thank your friend for the little things.** Whether that person shows up when you give a speech, play a game, or appear in a play, or even just drops off a few of your favorite desserts, let them know how much you appreciated their thoughtfulness. It's the little things over time that are long remembered and deserve a thank-you.

3. **Stay in touch.** While close friends, old friends, and childhood friends can go weeks, months, and sometimes even years without being in touch, don't wait that long. Check in on each other and connect. If someone is a friend you treasure, don't take them for granted, as you'll never know when it's too late. Reach out and catch up today.

CHAPTER 6

BONDING WITH YOUR FAMILY

"I want my family to be closer." Sound familiar? Perhaps you have that sentiment in common with all of us who want to foster and be a part of a close-knit, loving family. These bonds form the fabric of a life well lived, and family is the heartbeat that sustains us. Strengthening your family ties in meaningful ways occurs one day at a time, but it takes a lifetime of caring. The good news? It's worth it.

Every family is unique unto itself. Some of us have one whose bond is irrevocably tight. Others of us wish we could wave a magic wand and resolve any challenges. Now that I'm older, I realize *our* family is built on the strength of the bond between each member and can't be taken for granted. The responsibility for that bond also rests on my shoulders. As with every relationship in your life, if you make family your priority, you increase the chances of growing closer.

My parents were dedicated to building one big happy family. Their parents were the same way. They did everything possible to nurture togetherness. I have treasured memories of my parents and grandparents because we lovingly gathered for family dinners and holidays. I continue to ask myself, "How can I honor their legacy?" I have learned that it's by transmitting the love I received from them back into others. Out loud. We all hold the key to our own family bond.

This chapter addresses ways you can strengthen your family's togetherness. It takes time, effort, and caring beyond what's expected, especially when a problem doesn't have a simple solution, or family members need help or are unwilling to participate. No one said it would be easy. When loving out loud, you discover a newfound joy in making a little progress at a time. While it's not always possible to unite everyone in your family, family *is* forever and, in my book, worthy of your ongoing efforts.

Getting Closer All the Time

So let's get started. Family ties require an intentional effort to build the relationship. This means spending time together. Talking, catching up, and checking in on each family member. During happy times. Sad times. Challenging times. *Wishing* for a close family won't make it so; it takes time and energy.

Take Charge of Your Family History and Legacy

Become the family lineage holder. If preserving ancestral information is your priority, consider being the family bond builder, historian, or matriarch or patriarch, and welcome it as an opportunity to surround yourself with and get to know loved ones, past and present. One such person requested a few written pages about each family member's life story — their careers, successes, and milestones — and began putting together a family history. If your family is enormous, start with closest relatives and build from there.

Envisioning how you'd like your family to be is one thing. Putting that love into action and expressing it in a kind, thoughtful way is another. It's easy to point a finger at other family members or turn your head because you're too busy. Building a family bond takes a mix of traditions, sharing time together, and caring in good times, not just banding together when things get bad. Often, forgiveness is the central theme. Value each family member, and view them as a treasure trove of knowledge.

Strengthen the Bond

Psychologist Anthony Levitas weighed in on bond building:

When it comes to family, keep in mind it's all about sustaining the family bond. It's the innate knowledge that you know someone is there for you. Sometimes it's not blood family, but family becomes the individuals you choose to let into your life and share with intimately. If a situation is unhealthy and someone is toxic, it's about altering your expectations or even letting go when you come to a realization that you continue to be hurt over and over. Then it's time to emotionally disengage. In the end, it comes down to building a bond that's based on trust.

Here are some ways to begin building your family bond:

Get to know each family member one at a time. What is their passion? Their interests? When is their birthday or anniversary, and what significant life events should you remember? Most people don't even know each other's birthdays. Learn about their children and grandchildren or pets if they have any. Can you refer customers to their business? Getting to know each other is the goal, and consistently showing up is key.

Figure out your family values. If you don't know them and teach them by example, then how does the next generation learn what they are? Words passed on carry legacies of love. What does your family stand for, and how do you build loving-kindness? Does it make you proud to be a part of this family? How can you contribute?

Be the first. Be the first to call, make up, apologize, and work toward reconciliation with family members when possible. You only have one family; care for it like a rare treasure first and foremost.

Don't delay caring. Is a family member in need of more support? Whether you are a loved one's caregiver or someone in your family is ill, inquire how you can help give TLC. Perhaps share an audiobook, read out loud to an elderly relative who loves a good book, or provide a family member with their favorite music from when they were young. Schedule meals to be delivered that will help nourish them through their recovery, or volunteer to visit and create meaningful ways to spend time if someone is infirm.

Consider, also, the caregiver, who needs breaks and support, and spread your love and attention. You can never care enough, especially when someone is not well or is under the weather. If a family member is ill or lives in another city, talk to their primary caregiver and inquire how you can help. Sometimes it's as simple as calling regularly or helping coordinate extra care or support that is needed.

Select a family cause and support it. Perhaps a family member had a serious illness or cared about a significant nonprofit need in the community; volunteer at the local charity walk and support it in their honor or memory. There are many ways to volunteer together, build the bond, and do something purposeful in your family name.

Show up for each other. Learn ways you can support each other. Whether it's attending a child's sporting event or play, a speech that a family member is giving, or a ceremony honoring a loved one, those important moments become more meaningful with your attendance and support.

Reach out just because. Call a family member even when nothing is going on. In other words, just because you're thinking of them and care. Making a "just because" LOL call goes a long way. Do it often.

Update each other. Create a family calendar and list everyone's contact information and date of birth or marriage so you'll also know when there are extra-special occasions and birthdays. Spread the word, not just when something challenging happens but when there's happy news, too. Perhaps a family member got a job promotion or purchased a new home. A young person graduated from college, or a family member was honored for their volunteerism. Share ways family members can acknowledge each other.

Introduce family members to your family of friends.
Share your family with your friends, and vice versa, out
loud. Have a breakfast and include both. Host a dinner
party and invite your cousins along with your closest
friends. Bring friends and family together, bridging
two important parts of your life and your world. No-
tify both friends and family when a baby is born, and
share the parents' contact details so everyone sends
loving congratulations.

Welcome new members to the family. Plan a get-
together in their honor, volunteering to take part in the
entertaining; or call the happy couple when a relative
gets engaged, being especially attentive to the new family member. Put out the family welcome mat!

> **LOL:** Take a moment and think about your inten-
> tions for loving your family out loud. Wishing
> won't make a solid bond happen. Start small and
> reach out to a family member today with a hello,
> "I'm thinking of you," or "I love you."

Here are a few ways to get closer to your family by
sharing:

Share your family values. Brenda and her husband,
Ken, are very close to their daughters — who are also
close — as well as to the rest of the family. I asked how
as parents they built such a strong family unit, and
Brenda replied, "We tell our kids and family members,

'this is how our family does it.'" In other words, they are clear what works for them, and they have built the kind of family that is caring, thoughtful, and considerate. They are also extremely involved in their community and work hard to help the homeless, the schools their daughters attended, and an array of causes they are passionate about. If you are fortunate enough to be their friends, you feel as if you're also part of their family.

Schedule times to talk and listen. We are all busy and time flies. If you want to build a closer relationship with your teens, adult children, or family members who are always on the go, make it clear you'd like to talk on a regular basis, at the very least once a week. Schedule a lunch or share you'd like to hear from them more often. One father requested his son update him weekly about his new business, and it worked. He said, "Every Friday afternoon my son calls me, and I've been able to guide him and support him. These 'My Day Friday' calls have become something we both look forward to. They can be brief or longer, but it's our special talk time."

Offer your undivided attention. Another family demonstrated togetherness by planning a vacation that included no work. This mother and father of two saved up their days off and planned a spring-break staycation as a family. They discussed having a no-work week with the kids and giving them their undivided attention. They planned family outings, from nature walks to bowling to eating out and more. Later when their son was asked what his favorite vacation was, he instantly replied, "I loved the week we stayed home and spent every day together as a family with Mom and Dad's full attention."

Share the love you've received out loud. Christine Pullara shared her role-model inspiration for loving her family and children out loud, which she does generously: "My first and brightest influence for treating others with respect and love is my mother, Violet. Growing up I saw the positive impact she had on people regardless of their age, background, or social standing in life. She genuinely loves people, and that feeling is mutual. I think back on some of the challenges she endured during my childhood, and I'm amazed at how adept she was at staying positive and continuing to shine her light. She was and continues to be such a role model for me."

Christine added, "I feel loved when my family is all together and focused on each other. No electronics, just us doing simple things: playing a game while eating dinner, doing a puzzle, going for a walk!"

Share and honor family members' wisdom. While it can be difficult to be patient with a well-intentioned elder telling you what to do, what they learned when they were younger, and so on, if you open your heart and love out loud, you listen with love, too. Instead of being in a hurry, slow down and listen to their stories and sage advice. Ask yourself, *What can I learn?* Read between the lines. Family members who wish to share wisdom with us love us. They want to save us from the pain, disappointment, or suffering they perhaps went through in their lifetime of experiences. My best advice has come from generations before me. I even wish today I could have back some of those days with my parents, to sit down and listen with love. The wisdom of our elders and those who love us is golden. Treasure yours.

Have a Family Meeting

Psychologist Stephen Garber and his wife, Marianne, an educational consultant, practice together at the Behavioral Institute of Atlanta, helping families and children. They have conducted family meetings with their own four children since they were very young. They began these meetings weekly to talk about family values, getting organized for school, and working together as a family. Now that their kids are grown and married, they still have a yearly family meeting, updating everyone on finances and planning that will be helpful for each of them and their growing families to know. At the first adult meeting, the family collaborated to write a "Family Mission Statement" that expressed the values they hold dear. The family meeting continues to be an integral part of their lives and a loving way they build their own family bond.

An excerpt from the Garber Family Mission Statement reads: "As a family we strive to create a loving atmosphere that supports closeness, trust, and open communication within the immediate and extended family as well as across the generations. We believe that we need to make the world a better place by doing good, giving of our time, talent, and resources to help others in need, and act as responsible citizens of our community and world."

LOL: Envision the family you wish to become. Say what you mean and mean what you say. Share how you'd like your family to build and bond. Togetherness happens one hour, day, and month at a time.

Loving Your Family Out Loud

It's so easy to take our families for granted, but I have learned so much from my aunt Lois, who has become our go-to, adored family matriarch. She has served as a second mother to me my entire life, with her wisdom, caring, and abundance of unconditional love. She has consistently gone above and beyond for our entire family. When I think of how I can make a difference, I think of Aunt Lois as my role model and find ways to support our family.

All too often you see your family only at special

occasions or sad times when someone has passed away. I have tried in my own way to initiate more time together as a family. After my mother passed away, I invited everyone over, and we watched family movies and had a lovely dinner. These are cherished moments you can't get back. Mix traditions with something novel and fun, and share quality time together. Here are some memorable ideas that have worked for family members:

Create a Memory Box

This togetherness gift was priceless. On Lorraine Fleishman's ninetieth birthday, her daughter Cheryl flew home and surprised her. She rang the bell, and her mother — alias GG, for Great-Grandmother — was shocked and delighted. Cheryl posted the video online, and it was so touching.

As the ultimate gift of love, Cheryl presented GG with a beautiful box filled with letters and cards. She organized the gift by requesting that the entire family — including grandchildren, great-grandchildren, and cousins — share a memory. Cheryl wrote them, "It's Grandma's 90th! Let's tell her now how much we love her and share experiences, a special sentiment, and your birthday wish as she moves forward at 90!"

Seated at the kitchen table, Cheryl's mom opened each letter, one by one, and read it out loud. Tears flowed, and laughter filled the room. Cheryl's mother later shared that she repeatedly reads the letters and said it was the best gift she's ever gotten. A life of love, well lived!

Celebrate Traditions with Every Family Member

My childhood friend Gail has a very close family, including over 150 first, second, and third cousins. Her entire family has stayed in contact, even renting a large hall for family functions. One family member added a huge room to the house so it can hold everyone during religious holidays and special occasions. All the family members chip in for the meals. Talk about togetherness — this family wrote the book on it! A rule is that significant others must be married or engaged to come to family events. In other words, when a relative shows up with someone else, there's a ring on their finger, and everyone celebrates together as their family grows.

Cousins. Once a year or whenever possible, get all your cousins together if you live in the same city, and have a cousins' lunch. I have just started this with two of my cousins, and I look forward to it now as a yearly tradition. Everyone can bring a photograph of the cousins over the years and be prepared to laugh, cry, hear updates, and share favorite stories and memories.

Children. Be proud out loud. I'm so proud of my children that sometimes I could burst. Recently I was stopped by someone who told me about a good deed my son had done. I beamed with pride. I immediately called him and shared the compliment. He appreciated my call. A circular compliment is one that goes around, and it's also called good karma, as it circulates with a lot of love inside.

Grandchildren. Have an anything day! Invite your grandchildren over, and plan a day or afternoon with you where they select what they want to do. Within reason, see if you can follow through. It's a beautiful thing to give the gift of choice, and your shared time will be remembered. Brainstorm a list of "anything" activities, and be sure to include learning something new or doing something that is free and fabulous (for example, visiting the library, looking for four-leaf clovers, planting seeds in a garden or egg cartons, or gazing up at the sky and identifying all the shapes in the clouds). I gave a dinner party with the grandchildren in honor of Dr. Seuss on his birthday. We read his books, enjoyed a snack of Goldfish crackers, and had a fun time.

You can also grandparent across the miles. One devoted grandfather, Zayde Ed, reads a chapter book to his five-year-old and three-year-old grandsons on a video call. He keeps it short and picks up next time wherever he left off. It's a special time, and this tradition has continued for over two years now. He selects books that are age appropriate and exciting to read out loud. The grandsons enjoy their grandfather's reading time, and it has become a special way he stays connected, sharing time, fun memories, and a love of reading across the miles.

Sisters. Three sisters have a travel tradition. They go on a spa vacation to the same favorite location every year, bring the latest beauty products and favorite books with duplicates for each sister, and share life-enhancing tips with updates on how to have the best life possible. Following each trip, because these ideas, insights, tips, and recipes are all so informative and smart, they publish a little "Sisterly Love" newsletter and share it with family and friends each year as their holiday card.

Brothers. Our grandson was born on the same day as his older brother, three years apart. Preparing the big brother to "brother" was important, so he was given some jobs, like being in charge of saying good night, offering hello hugs to family coming to visit, and sharing what his baby brother has been doing and dreaming about. Brotherly love is so special — capture it with a together photo of brothers on every birthday. One family celebrates "Brotherly Love" day, and all the brothers in their family go out to dinner and catch up on each other's lives.

Aunts and uncles. My aunts and uncles have always been like second parents. Staying in touch with them is a gift you give yourself as well. If you are lucky enough to be a niece or nephew, consider ways you

can celebrate your aunt or uncle. Find out what they
love to eat, be it roasted almonds or a special family
recipe you bake, and drop off a sampling. Share time
together reminiscing about priceless family memories
and stories they might remember. When one gentleman's uncle passed away, he had cards made that said,
"What would Uncle Martin do?" Everyone went to
this family member for his sage advice, and the card
reminded them to keep consulting his memory. Aunts
and uncles are such special people. Treasure yours.

Parents. Be happy together and clap the loudest! Many
parents spend much of their lives cheering on and
supporting their children. When the tables are turned,
and children show support for their parents, it's truly
meaningful. My beloved sister-in-law, Esther Levine,
a well-known escort for visiting authors and celebri-
ties in Atlanta, is credited with having initiated and
founded the Marcus Jewish Community Center of
Atlanta's Book Festival. Her son, his wife, and her
grandson flew down from New York for the evening
when Esther was being honored. She was so thrilled
they attended, and it made Esther's honor even sweeter.
For us, it was such a joy to share in and witness a family's pride in their amazing mother.

Quote Loved Ones

In my friend Gail's family, when you ask her father,
who is called Papa Leon, how he is doing, he replies,

"Never better." We all quote Papa Leon, as that answer sums up how a beloved grandfather makes the best of every day by cheering up everyone else around him. He's certainly an inspiration.

Ellen just lost her mother, who was ninety-four years old. Her mother had a very difficult life, having lost her own parents and her siblings at a very early age. Ellen told me, "My mother always said, 'You know how much I love you.'" For most that would be framed as a question, but in this case, it was a statement. She explained that her entire life her mother made sure she knew she was loved unconditionally, and she never tired of hearing that sentiment. Now that her mother has passed, Ellen continues to share this practice with her children, and these simple words of love are passed down.

Compute This!

Technology has made it possible to be endlessly creative while still loving out loud. While I suggest not relying only on technology to share your emotions, it's certainly convenient and relevant to the times. If you want to share your feelings and affection for a family member across the miles or everyone in your family is busy, "show up" online. Emailing a "virtual" cake in their honor, posting signs on social media, or a group Skype call singing "Happy Birthday" or any song your kids learn at school — or just saying "we love you" — can be meaningful and fun. Sharing little tech-savvy

LOL moments is ideal when you are short on time but long on loving.

What's cooking? A devoted mom named Gennie loved to cook with her own mom and now continues the tradition with her daughter Jasmine. With digital photography and recipes easily found online, she is teaching Jasmine to cook and creating an at-home gluten-free cookbook, since they share that dietary need in common. Their mother-daughter cookbook keeps growing and is becoming a treasured "healthy" keepsake.

Here are some fun virtual ways to send your love and share your feelings:

- Make video dates online to share time together (such as a grandparent reading an age-appropriate book out loud to a grandchild, sisters planning a holiday get-together, and so forth). With a little tech support, everyone can get connected and stay in touch. Think of something positive to share, from good news to how your day was to even a funny knock-knock joke the children will love repeating.
- Use technology to bridge family. If someone is absent because they are unable to attend a family gathering, connect with that family member online to include them. My mother fell and broke her hip the week before a family wedding, and we arranged for her to watch the ceremony from her nursing-home bed. We recorded it as well and gathered by her side watching it a second time the next day.

- Share a theme song that expresses your feelings. From "We Are Family" to "I Just Called to Say I Love You," there are many wonderful choices to musically express your feelings. One mom taught her adorable daughter to sing "Happy Birthday" to her niece on her birthday. She taped it on her phone and shared it out loud, which was heartwarming and priceless. This perfect greeting was music to her ears!

- Capture and share a moment. From across the miles, our daughter-in-law Alicia sends the cutest photographs of our grandson Scott at preschool, including getting his backpack ready, singing, and participating in programs. We revisit those photo-op moments repeatedly for an instant smile.

- Have a virtual family book club. One mom I know shares a new book each month with her daughters and daughters-in-law, and they have a group conference call to discuss it. It's a special time shared, and every month they take turns selecting a book to read.

- Remember the five o'clock virtual call. Every day at five, since he was a small boy, my friend's son has called and connected online with his grandmother in another city to say hello. Those five o'clock calls have kept them very close over the years. If it was five o'clock, it was Grandma time on the phone or online.

- Help family and friends go online. Be someone

who supports a family member or friend whom you consider your extended family to go online. Whether it's teaching tech-savvy skills to help someone special to you shine at work or improve their online dating life, offer your know-how. When it comes to building computer skills, and especially putting up a profile online, they might need some assistance, new photographs, and your encouragement. Sometimes all someone needs is a little push in the right direction. Be mine online!

When sharing sensitive feelings, especially ones that might be perceived as negative or critical, avoid posting them online or sending reactive texts or emails, which might suit you during the moment but can be harmful to your relationship. Those rapid-fire words, or even ones you carefully craft, might be very hurtful to someone who may have meant well, inadvertently made an error, or didn't see them coming. There are kind ways to share your feelings out loud, giving someone the opportunity to respond, and achieve a positive outcome. Also, when the moment feels right, talk with the individual and request an opportunity to discuss situations that might be delicate one-on-one.

Creating Dinnertime LOL Memories

Meals are a special time even if you can manage only a few organized family dinners a week. Dinnertime is a shared opportunity to truly connect and build new memories with every bite. If possible, discuss your family meals and create a list of healthy favorites that you can all agree on and look forward to.

Technology-free dinners. One family with three teenagers shared their family rule that everyone's cell phones are turned off at dinner unless there's something urgent happening. That way, the meal isn't interrupted by hearing all the phones ring at every bite, and family members aren't racing through to check messages. It's understood family is the main course and deserves everyone's undivided attention.

A feast of love. One newly married couple has spaghetti and meatballs every Friday night. They frequently invite family members, and it's a special time to share their tradition. They both love to cook but work and have very little time, so it's also an easy dinner to prepare and throw together. Another family celebrates the Shabbat together, while yet another spends the first Sunday of every month eating out at a different restaurant. The only criteria are that the restaurant be kid friendly and have a kids' menu so little ones enjoy it, too.

> **LOL:** As the kids leave home and your family spreads out, plan holiday meal celebrations to look forward to, even if they're months away.

Family mealtime topics. By offering conversation starters and sharing your own answers, you can role-model healthy and positive ways to talk about the things that matter. Brainstorm ideas for game night, outings, or other ways your family can play together. Discuss news in your family members' and their friends' lives. Talk about current events and world news to stay informed.

While every family dinner won't include all these topics, consider a few to address while eating together:

- "What's wonderful about your life this week?"
- "What challenges can you share?"
- "Is there anyone we know who needs our time, help, and attention?"
- "What's the funniest thing that happened today?"
- "How were you or someone else helpful or kind today?"
- "Do you have anything you need our family's help with?"
- "How can we build togetherness and make some plans together?"

> **LOL:** Create family-meal themes, whether the kids plan or cook the meal, or you make a new recipe to taste-test it. Also, prepare Grandma's treasured recipes everyone loves.

Grand Grandparenting

Becoming a grandparent is one of life's greatest gifts. Sharing in the lives of your children and their children and loving your grandkids out loud is simply delicious.

Grandparenting is everything it's cracked up to be and more. Much more. My grandchildren and I have bonded over art projects, story time, dance parties, playing games on the floor, and outings to the park. The time we share is golden, and it's one of the most beautiful privileges in life to be a grandparent. As an aunt or uncle or another close relative, it's also special to deem yourself Grand-Aunt or Grand-Uncle — especially if, like me, you think a child is the grandest gift of all.

A lasting way to love someone out loud is the bestowing of names on newborns in memory or honor of a loved one such as a grandparent. Each religion and culture approaches this in a different way, and often a ceremony talks about the person or those beloved family members a baby is named after. That honor is one of the most beautiful ways a person lives on in our hearts and minds. Put the reason for the naming in writing, read it out loud, and commemorate the occasion.

LOL Grandparent Names and Special Requests

Another significant moment is deciding what name a new grandmother or grandfather will go by. We get to choose our name, or sometimes a family member or child starts calling us a name and it sticks. In my case, my daughter Ali named me Ro Ro. I loved it, and that became my name. Now when my grandchildren say my name, I melt. It's truly one of the most beautiful ways to love someone out loud to call them by their name, especially when you're a grandparent!

Choose your grandparent name with care and make it memorable! A creative name goes a long, long way and will put a smile on your face every time you hear it. Your grandparenting name is like a hug out loud. It can symbolize someone who is sweet, giving, and loving — for instance, "my marshmallow daddy," which is what I called my father, of blessed memory; or "Honey," my dear friend Patty's grandparent name. Patty's husband, Larry, had her name put on a license plate, proudly displayed on her car. Here comes Honey!

Suggest a grandparent name. In my case, my name, Robyn, was proclaimed by my daughter to be Ro Ro, in keeping with my aunt Lois's name, which was Lo Lo. I taught the grandchildren my name by singing "Row, Row, Row Your Boat." And frequently I ask, "Are you ready to Ro Ro?" when we're heading out for an afternoon of fun. *Glam-ma*, *Mama Dear*, *Papa Dear*, *Mimi*, *Nana*, *Mamaw*, *Pops*, *Tops*: your own little language of love makes it fun to share your special bond out loud.

Put in a "grandparent" LOL request. Since everyone is busy, as a gentle reminder, I suggested to my adorable six-year-old granddaughter Dani that I had a "Ro Ro request" that I'd love for her to think about. I shared, "If you have not spoken to me in seven days, please call, connect online, or come see me." Dani instantly agreed. When she was getting picked up after playing at our house, she repeated the request to her mom, who graciously agreed to facilitate it. While we all talk and see each other often, it means so much to know we're thinking of each other — it's the thought that counts, after all! — and not a week goes by without connecting.

Video grandparent thank-yous. *You've got mail!* When Marcia, a dedicated grandmother of two toddlers, lovingly sends a package to her grandchildren in another city, her daughter-in-law records the kids opening it. She sends the video back to Marcia, and it's such a wonderful way to say "thank you." Marcia's grandchildren's excitement when opening her packages is priceless. The laughter and love displayed in the cell-phone videos warm Marcia's heart. Her packages are a major hit, and she loves sending these surprises as much as the little ones love opening them.

LOL Snapshot

When at thirteen my daughter Ali did not get chosen in a cheerleading dance squad competition, she was very disappointed. She had gotten to the final round and was the last dancer cut. A bit unsure how to handle her disappointment, I recalled that my grandmother Pauline had an open-mic gathering for the residents at her nursing home that day. I drove Ali to see her. While she was sitting with my grandmother, they asked if anyone else had a talent, and

Ali volunteered to get up and dance. Half the audience was sleeping in their wheelchairs, and for some reason when she started dancing, they all woke up, and the entire room began clapping and cheering for her. It meant the world to my grandmother that we came, and she was so proud of Ali, who ultimately enjoyed it most of all. She loved dancing for her grandma, and the entire room returned the love that day, which put a smile on her face and everyone else's.

Honoring Our Parents, Our Families, and Past Generations

There's often a someone who is the family historian, keeper of your family records, or relative who seems to stay in touch with everyone and serve as the glue that keeps the family together. While a generation before me, and those before them, captured our family tree, I have served as the current keeper of the family history, documenting it for generations to come.

When my parents died, I also inherited their high school annuals, thousands of photographs, and countless mementos. I treated every item with the same TLC they gave these objects while they were alive. It took me almost two years to carefully sort through everything; share photographs with cousins, other relatives, and the local heritage museum; and contact everyone I felt would appreciate the keepsakes. To preserve these mementos, I did the following:

- Framed my father's World War II medals and badges.

- Preserved my mother's pink wooden baby hanger that her own mother had saved, which is now over ninety years old. It has a baby on it and is one of the sweetest keepsakes ever. I look forward to giving it to my daughter Ali when she has a baby.

- Wrapped a silk ribbon around decades' worth of my mother's cherished love letters from my father that shall remain unopened. The large stack reminds me of their enormous love for and devotion to each other.

- Placed mementos, photographs, and the *New York Times* announcement of the wedding of my mother to my father in a console topped with a glass shadow box at our home's entry. This idea was lovingly inspired by Barbara Garber, who beautifully preserved her own family treasures in a glass-top enclosed shelf.

- Donated historical references, including important letters and deeds, and interesting photographs of my great-grandparents to the Breman Museum in Atlanta, which stored them on film for future generations. The photographs were fragile, and I was able to turn in the history of each one after I spent weeks ensuring the collection remained intact and was preserved.

- Saved a Howdy Doody toy, manufactured by my dad in the 1950s, in a plexiglass box as one of my treasures from childhood. It plays "Happy Birthday"

and a few other songs and is among my most beloved reminders of my father's endless creativity.

- Created a display cabinet for my mother's china
dalmatian collection, which began over forty years
ago as she and I went antiquing every month. I now
have a collection of over one hundred little china
dogs of different origins, and each represents time
spent with my mom. Many were gifts I bought for
her as we "spotted" these spotted dogs reminiscent
of the dalmatians I grew up with and loved over
the years, including Pokey, Smokey, and later, Dice.

> **LOL:** Think of ways to allow your loved ones'
> treasured keepsakes and memories to live on.
> Select a few items that serve as constant loving
> reminders of generations past, and incorporate
> them into your life or home to be passed down
> through the years.

Ways to Honor Loved Ones

As my aunt shared years ago, we're all going to be hit in
life. Either in the beginning, the middle, or later, in the
end. I was in my twenties when we lost our first close
family member, my beloved grandma Annie, and it was
on the day before my best friend's wedding. I kept my
promise, as my grandmother would have wanted, and
walked down the aisle as her maid of honor but didn't
stay for the wedding celebrations. To date, I have lost
many dear, amazing family members and friends and

care deeply about honoring each of their memories. The love they poured into me has now spilled into my family and friends, as that love can never die, especially when shared.

Keep the love alive. That is my loving-out-loud mantra. When I call an elderly cousin or someone my mom and dad adored, I know my parents would be pleased, and I envision them being proud that I am a caring individual. I do it in their loving memory and reap more love back than I could ever give. I try to continue showing the same compassion they would have done had they been alive. That keeps me in touch with them. When someone passes, it gives us the opportunity to share that love they poured into us with others, and the ripple of love continues. That's why I believe love does not die.

Honor the tears. When my mother died, I was lost. I asked the rabbi, "Why do we cry, and what is the importance of crying?" Of course, I thought I knew the answer, but I didn't expect what he said, which motivated a deeper understanding of tears. I learned, contrary to my previous notion, that tears are the soul's response to a profound experience. We should always ask ourselves, "What do we have to care about to the extent that we'll cry?" This question will help us define our values, set our priorities, and direct our spiritual growth.

Here's the eulogy I gave for my mother:

If Phyllis Freedman loved you, you were *loved out loud*. You knew she was proud of you. Happy to see you. She cared daily about what was going on in your life. The world had the gift of our mom for eighty-seven years. And what a gift. I loved her stories. I loved sharing my life with her. I loved it when she said I should cut my hair an inch or she liked my outfit. I loved listening to her Port Chester, New York, childhood stories, and I loved watching her play solitaire and the piano, and I simply loved her inside and out.

Mom taught me there is nothing in this world that is too hard if you try. And at the very least, you'd know you tried. It would be understandably difficult to let go of a gift like my mom, even later in life, so today I'm making it clear. I will miss her madly, but her presence will always be with me.

I recently was told that "the best part of us is never born, and the best part of us will never die." I can only pray the best of my mother lives on in me and each of us. What a wonderful world that would be.

LOL: Understand what you loved about departed family members. To honor your loved one who is no longer with you, see how to emulate their best character traits yourself. Do not resist the tears that honor your love for someone you cared about deeply.

Treasure the Family Tree

I was very fortunate to inherit a well-documented family tree on one side. Sharing your tree with your entire family and updating it over time is a gift that loves your relatives, even your ancestors, out loud.

If you or anyone in your family is willing to do this, I highly recommend it. Robert Faneuil, a father and grandfather dedicated to preserving his family history, is an advocate for researching our family origins and ancestry: "We all (male and female, siblings and parents) should do DNA testing. It opens a whole new world. If you get one hit, it may provide you with the answer to your questions or provide you with photos or lead you to another person. We owe it to our ancestors."

Robert taught himself to preserve family history online. Here are some ways for you to build a family tree:

Use any of the online genealogy resources. Robert prefers Ancestry.com because of the voluminous records available.

Call each family member and get children's names and birth dates correct. Then find a family tree illustration (online) to fill in, and even if you do a little at a time, get started!

Once the family tree is completed, make everyone copies and send it out. Include one request: As our family grows, please alert us all and add each new member to the tree.

Create a family album. One family requested every member write two pages of pertinent information about themselves, their parents, family, and life. The purpose was to document for future generations their life and legacy. All the stories were supplemented with family photographs, backgrounds, and more. The family collectively contributed money to get the book typeset and printed and had a book-launch party with each family member signing their page. They also contributed favorite family recipes that everyone treasured and prepared and served them at the party. Anyone who wanted to learn to cook one of the recipes could also join family members to learn how to make it.

When There's a Breakup

Often there are family members who are divorced, estranged, or legally separated. Or a loved one passes, and their spouse remarries.

When this happens, while sometimes it presents a challenge, it does not have to make your personal relationship more difficult. Even following a couple's split, many family members stay very close with the ex-spouse, especially when children and grandchildren are involved. While you are probably closer to one side because you are related by blood, caring about the well-being of former family members does not have to stop. In life when a new normal is our only option, we can be bitter or better. Choose better.

Acknowledge both parties. Consider leaving a message or sending a card to say that you are sorry a couple is breaking up. Regardless of why, in most cases, letting both parties know you care about them is important for the present and future. While a couple might not get along at first, there's always hope for the future goal of everyone being amicable, and the sooner that happens, the better, especially for the sake of children.

Know that it's never too late. A unique story was shared by an ex-sister-in-law who wished to reunite after many years with her former husband's sister. She pretended to do an "ex" vanishing party so she and her previous sister-in-law would be sisters again. After many years, they are back together and cherish their newfound relationship, both grateful to have each other back in their lives. Reach out to family members who are splitting up or getting a divorce. You don't have to get involved; rather, just say you'll miss seeing them or you are sorry to learn the news. Words of kindness matter most, and you can never do wrong by doing right.

Doing Your Share of the Giving

This chapter ends on the notion that you shouldn't wait for your family members to contact you to say hello or catch up or get connected. If you are waiting for an invitation or for them to reach out, you are standing on ceremony. Do your share of the giving, and perhaps even more, to jump-start a relationship. Holding a grudge or being stubborn gets you nowhere. It's easy to show up and reach out, but sometimes family members are not receptive to your love. While there are some families or family members who can't love out loud or, sadly, even get along, forgiving family or asking for forgiveness, when possible, is a gift you give yourself and generations to come.

> **LOL:** Don't postpone cultivating closeness. Do not take your family for granted. There are many ways to bond with your family; don't delay.

Three LOL Things You Can Do Today to Bond with Your Family

1. **Remember the power of one.** Build your family bond and connection one family member at a time. You don't just grow close to entire family instantly; it requires getting to know each family member and investing time and thought, with the intention to love out loud.

2. **Establish traditions.** Even if it's just once a year at a cousins' lunch or an unbirthday party or a family dinner, stay in touch. Create new traditions or preserve ones from years past. Family reunions are

wonderful, but don't wait for one to get together. Yearly traditions keep your family united.

3. **Stand for something as a family.** Understand your family values, and love your family out loud at every opportunity by instilling these values in your lives. Make a difference and keep family members' legacies alive by giving back in their memory.

CHAPTER 7

LOVING OUT LOUD AT WORK, BY VOLUNTEERING, AND ON THE GO

The character each of us brings to our work, volunteering, or anything we do in life says a lot about us. Whether you work from home, commute to a full-time job, or volunteer, your work, when purposeful, can be a wonderful opportunity to live and give of your best self out loud. And *love* it.

This chapter shares ways to purposefully and meaningfully connect at work, giving our time, talents, or treasures, whether it's career related or volunteering. Some professions require a large dose of empathy; however, being compassionate wherever we go helps us connect to something greater than ourselves. When we show up as a caring coworker, a devoted employee, a passionate volunteer, and someone who looks for ways to brighten the lives of others, *our* lives become purpose filled. When we take on another person's burden as if it were our own, we lift each other up.

Like most of us, you likely spend a large part of your life working, so infuse it with purpose no matter what you do or where. You never know another person's story, and we all get hit sometime in life, so bring your heart to work. Over the years my work has led me to new contacts and friendships, and volunteering has broadened my horizons and enlivened my outlook immeasurably. This chapter will share the insights of individuals from all walks of life who have found meaning in their work and lives by loving out loud.

The Business of Kindness

Whether you own a business or work for someone else or from home, you can be in the business of kindness, bring your best self wherever you go, and in the process transform your life at work. From initiating an employee volunteer program at your place of business to mentoring another or asking to be mentored by someone you admire, you can have an impact at your workplace.

Joey Reiman, author of *The Story of Purpose*, was named by *Fast Company* as one of the one hundred people who will change the way the world thinks. Joey shared:

Make a loving, not a living. Ask yourself three questions: (1) *What do I love?* (2) *What am I good at?* and (3) *How can it help another?* The key to these questions is the order. First you need to love what you do. You can learn to be good at just about anything, but loving what you do is all-important. Lastly, all we have is what we can give away. The best way to wake up in the morning is with a why! People can dictate who you talk to, where you will work, when you need to be somewhere, and how much they will pay you. But no one can take your why away. Define yourself, or you will be defined. The purpose of life is to live your life on purpose.

Recently, a gentleman shared how he admired a company of the past whose name was IXL. The company and its name stood for its motto of excellence, "I Excel." Think about your signature style when it comes to your own work ethic. Here are a few promises I make to myself that inspire me daily:

- *Show up kinder than necessary.*
- *Overdeliver and do my best.*
- *Leave things better than I found them and envision the way things should be, every single day.*

What's your work ethic? Create a mission statement and stick to it. Review it at the end of each day and ensure that you're on track being the kind of person you want to be more often.

Create a Personal Philosophy

When Silicon Valley customer engagement executive Shira Levine left the company where she worked for a move, her senior vice president asked her to share her personal philosophy with the team. She generously did so with the whole company, and here's a sampling of Shira's Top Ten:

1. Give your time, smarts, love, and friendship freely. We are all in this together.
2. Don't wait until you're 48 to let what's on the inside show on the outside.
3. Manners matter! Always say "please" and "thank you."
4. Every decision is about the client. What will they love? If you're unsure, ask your customer support team.
5. Encourage radical sharing and vulnerability. Especially when developing/working on something new.
6. Lead! Don't be afraid to lead. You're a warrior.
7. Deliver one sincere compliment per day.
8. When you act transparently and speak sincerely, people will see your point.
9. Fight for your opinion, in a polite way. Also, invite debate. Allow yourself to be proven wrong and *love it* when you are.
10. Give others credit.

Harry Maziar, a retired CEO and president of a large chemical company, shared his feelings following his decades of making a difference during his career: "There's a prominent place for kindness in business. You catch more flies with honey than you do with vinegar. Kindness translates into relationships by thinking, *What's in it for them?* rather than *What's in it for me.*" Harry added, "If you do good…you'll do well."

When my father retired, dismantled his office, and packed everything up, there was a bulletin board still hanging with a poem posted on it called "Good Business." It was his philosophy that spoke volumes to me. I took it down and kept it for years. It continues to remind me of what really matters in life and at work.

Good Business

The reason people pass one door…
To patronize another store,
Is not because the busier place…
Has better silks, or gloves, or lace
Or cheaper prices, but it lies…
In pleasant words and smiling eyes;
The only difference, I believe,
Is in the treatment folks receive.

— EDGAR A. GUEST

Practice the Golden Rule

Every time I run into my first producer, Spring Asher, I thank her for the role she played in my media career. It became crystal clear where this bright woman and role model gets her generous spirit, as recently I learned about her father, Bill Savitt, who lived to ninety-four and was a business legend in Hartford, Connecticut, with lessons to share. He credited the Young Judean club, an early boys' club that he belonged to as a youth, as a major influence. Members pledged to be good citizens, and it was there he learned to follow the Golden Rule. As a jewelry-store owner for sixty-eight years, he treated his customers as precious gems and earned endless accolades as a philanthropist and civic leader.

While his awards for his community leadership were extensive, his business practices were visionary. Yearly, Bill bought a block of concert tickets for the Connecticut Institute for the Blind, enabling students to hear the Hartford Symphony Orchestra. In 1987, he was chairman of his local Red Cross at the time of a major Connecticut flood and had an impact on the economic recovery policies. The governor proclaimed a Bill Savitt Day and, at the end of his career, named a street after him, Savitt Way.

Bill was best known for his business and advertising motto "P.O.M.G.," which stood for "Peace of mind guaranteed." A quarter century later, his grandson

Richard First named his company POMG Bike Tours of Vermont, and stands by his grandfather's customer service promise, "To give each customer a great experience."

What sums up Bill's life best is the Golden Rule: "Do unto others as you would have others do unto you." Bill Savitt believed in humanity's most cherished rule and gave out "Golden" rulers engraved with people's names to deserving folks who were good citizens.

What do you stand for? Create your own business motto and work and live by it. To create a compassionate workplace is good business. A well-known adage sums up compassion: "We make a living by what we get. We make a life by what we give." Whether you are the CEO, a manager, an employee, or a volunteer, you can have an impact on your place of business and wherever you go in life. A compassionate workplace is one that feels like a family, not just a business. Treat your employees like your customers. Honor volunteers in the same way, with gratitude, kindness, and appreciation. All of that spells love.

When someone is sick or going through a challenge, compassionate leaders and coworkers look for ways to help. Go the extra mile for a coworker, and check in and check up on each other. The same goes if you are a volunteer, as you are part of something greater than each of us working to make a difference.

Compassion means showing empathy and avoiding

being judgmental. Arianne loved her job but started to leave early each day due to extreme headaches. A coworker made a snide remark, commenting on how she was always cutting out of work early. Arianne finally got up the courage to speak up and asked her coworker for help. She said, "When I shared that I was having a hard time, my coworker was grateful that I shared this information. She immediately apologized for judging me, and we've been friends ever since. Now when I am under the weather or she is going through something, too, we cover for each other and it really helps."

Remember, it's often the little things that help others at work:

- Share ideas for understanding the lay of the land at work and who does what.
- Help someone at work with shortcuts that save valuable time.
- Share weather advice or commuting tips that might make someone's day easier.
- Remind someone if there's a meeting or important date to schedule or attend.
- Help a coworker get organized if you already have a list of important contacts.
- Celebrate coworkers' and your workplace's anniversaries. Show pride out loud for the length of time you and others have worked at a company.
- Be quick to be kind, instead of judging others.

LOL: Think about the person you bring to work. Judge no one. None of us really know what someone else is going through. Pitch in and see how you can help, especially before drawing any judgmental conclusions. Learn how to ask for help when needed, and know what you stand for at work.

It's Everyone's Job

If we each brighten our corner of the world, the whole world will be a brighter place. At work or at play, in business or at home, our actions affect others. It's everyone's job to care about the environment, which begins with us.

Reflect for a moment how our actions cause other people to work harder. Consider "If" at work as a vital part of *l-if-e*:

- If you throw a piece of paper down, who picks it up?
- If you leave a dirty coffee cup in the break room, who washes it and puts it away?
- If you don't put clothing back on its hanger in a dressing room, how does it get back to the store's floor inventory?
- If you leave trash at the cash register or on your desk, what happens to it?
- If you take up two parking spaces, how does that affect another person?

"Hanging" with Ed. A simple example of "it's everyone's job" is customer based but rings true for all of us, no matter where we work or go. Whenever my husband is at a store, he carefully hangs everything he tries on back up on the hanger and places it directly back on the rack where he found it. When Ed was growing up, his father had a retail store, and he knows how much work it is to take care of the items for sale. His intentions are kind and loving, as he also asks every restaurant we visit to use recyclable paper straws versus plastic, making his concern for the landfills and oceans apparent. Ed does not miss an opportunity to help others with his talents and skills, such as by repairing a friend's door with a broken hinge, and shares his love out loud with the little things that save other people time and energy.

From morning to night, consider: how can you compassionately make someone else's job and work life easier? Bring that same philosophy to work and wherever you go shopping.

All-aboard giving. As you are out and about, there are always ways to be helpful to others as well. Recently, while riding on a campus bus, a college student noticed all the trash that was being left on board and helped the driver pick it up after every route since he was the last passenger. The student started a campaign to reduce littering and inspired other students to "take your trash with you." He made a huge difference for this bus driver, who shared how he is able to get home a little earlier to tuck his kids in at night since his bus is now clean as a whistle.

Caring for our environment. Show your love and concern for Mother Earth. Contribute to reducing, recycling, and repurposing. From considering your environmental footprint to exploring how your workplace can recycle and reduce waste, being helpful can take on endless meanings at work or on the go. Keep in mind that it's everyone's job to be conscientious about conservation. What have you done lately for our environment?

Teamwork Makes the Dream Work

An employee new to a company wanted to share how excited she was to join the office. She started a list of reasons she liked it there and shared it with a coworker, who added his reasons, and the "chain letter" eventually exceeded one hundred entries. Here's a little snippet of the list.

I love my job because…

1. I work with generous people who are considerate of others.
2. Coworkers ask me if I am lost and offer to help.
3. We remember each employee birthday with a cupcake on their desk and a balloon.
4. It's everyone's job to pick up trash if we see it on the floor.

5. If someone does not understand a task, a coworker is only a desk away, ready to assist.

...and the list goes on!

Show Sincere Interest in Your Coworkers

Work friendships make your time at your job more enjoyable. It adds meaning to have work buddies, and these relationships can transform the workplace. Every individual at work has a story. When you pursue learning it, you make a connection that offers the opportunity to build a bond between you and that coworker.

Ask your coworkers, "What's your story?" If they are not forthcoming with details because they feel it's too personal, ask if they have any pets, scan their desk for photographs of their family, or notice what they seem interested in. Paying attention will connect you and can jump-start a friendship.

Remember the power of hello. While you might consider the anonymity of a larger workplace a challenge, everyone there is serving the same company. Saying hello opens the door to getting to know someone, especially at work. When you are the first to offer a greeting to a new employee, you open up that possibility, and it can be meaningful. Then listen. Notice if they have someone to eat lunch with and include them: "Hi, I don't know your name, but mine is Jason Smith, and I'm so happy to welcome you."

Work Etiquette Matters

Workplace etiquette is often not clear, and it is essential to understand the culture where you work. Find out from your HR representative, a fellow employee in your department, or someone who has been at the office a long time what the protocol is as it relates to gift giving, celebrating holidays, and more. Get the etiquette lay of the land.

Here are some things to consider:

- Does this office celebrate holidays, and how are they treated?
- Is there a committee that addresses special days; company anniversaries; and employee illnesses, family losses, and occasions like the birth of a new baby?
- Are there group gifts for the boss, or is gift giving off-limits or a personal, individual decision?
- Are there dress-down days or special company traditions you can participate in or institute?
- Is there a kindness committee or initiative to create a compassionate workplace? (If it is not apparent, ask if you can help initiate it with a like-minded group.)
- How do you thank your customers, coworkers, or volunteers? A thank-you at work goes a long way. Consider how your brand can stand for kindness, and share your gratitude and love out loud.

> **LOL:** The culture of your workplace is important to know, as it affects you and the way coworkers relate to each other. Inspire your company to add simple things like recognizing birthdays (if permissible) or special accomplishments, as well as supporting others during tough times.

Make a Difference a Day

Every morning before you go to work, say out loud, "Today I will make a difference." Consider all the ways you can help, chip in, and make someone else's day better or contribute in positive, productive ways. At the end of each day, ask yourself if you indeed made a difference.

Emily Hutmacher, a nonprofit executive, adds:

Giving is important because it's something that we all need at different times in life. We all have a basic need to feel connected and can do so by helping others. We need others to also invest in us in different ways throughout life, and giving comes in many forms, not just dollars. Giving time, expertise, guidance, and mentoring feeds the human spirit and unites people across varying circumstances who might otherwise never connect. Having worked in hospice care and among seniors, it seems most people want one thing to be certain when they die: to know without a doubt that they have made a meaningful difference for others here on Earth. Every day you are here on Earth, you are granted that powerful opportunity.

Some ways to make a difference

- Bring an extra umbrella if it's pouring or looks like it will pour. Offer it to a coworker who might have forgotten theirs.
- Put a flower in a vase on a friend's desk, and tell her you thought she might appreciate looking at something pretty to brighten her day.
- Share a little treat you bake or purchase and think your coworkers would enjoy.
- Keep a jar on your desk at work, and fill it with candies. Encourage your coworkers to enjoy them if they have a chocolate craving or sweet-tooth emergency. Or put a container in the break room, and everyone can take a turn choosing the treat of the month that's their favorite.

Be Somebody's Cheerleader

A large company wanted to personalize its recognition program, and each division assigned one volunteer to oversee the sunshine committee. It was this person's job to build a committee internally in their department with the responsibility of finding out if a coworker's family member was ill; someone had been out sick, had a baby, or experienced a recent death in the family; or anything else that deserved a hug, a smile, or a card expressing congratulations or sympathy. If an employee would benefit from a greeting card or a pretty flower on their desk, a budget was allocated to this effort to brighten their day at work.

Ways to cheer for others at work and make everyone's job easier

- Praise others without any ulterior motive.
- Tell the boss what a great job a coworker did, and be specific.
- Do not expect praise just because you give it. Offer sincere recognition to others because it's the right thing to do.
- Welcome someone new to the office, and inquire if there's anything you can do to assist them. Have an open-door policy if anyone needs your help.
- Collect nearby restaurant menus or list local resources for coworkers if they are new to the company.
- Be a Secret Santa year-round and leave little notes or surprises on someone's desk. You'll enjoy it as much as they will.
- Invite a colleague or coworker to lunch and get to know him or her.

> **LOL:** Consider yourself part of the team, and take responsibility for trying to keep the workplace a happy place to work.

Celebrate Your Customers, Coworkers, and Service Providers

Everyone is your customer. When you take that view of work, you realize that every person you meet matters. Each has the power to spread the word about your goods or services or whatever your business is, and when you take the time to truly make others feel special and important, you leave a wonderful impression.

Appreciate one customer at a time. At a restaurant I visited recently, the chef and co-owner went around the room ensuring each meal was to the customer's liking. The chef also learns a lot from these table-side visits, observing what's being enjoyed and how his cooking fares transport from kitchen to table. We've been back to that restaurant repeatedly, we look forward to seeing him, and it feels like one big happy family. Are you checking up on *your* customers, volunteers, or coworkers? Call it table-hopping, schmoozing, or being customer friendly — *I* call it smart.

> **LOL:** Build loyalty at work by showing respect and gratitude for your customers and everyone you come in contact with daily. Remember, everyone you meet or work with is significant. Everyone counts.

We are surrounded by an endless list of hardworking individuals — doctors, dentists, nurses, teachers, lawyers, waste-management workers, postal workers —

who go to great lengths to lighten our load in life or help us in myriad ways. Consider the individuals in your life who make a difference.

LOL Snapshot

A woman noticed her postal carrier in his truck around lunchtime when she was retrieving her mail on a hot summer day. She greeted him and asked why he didn't have lunch, and he replied that he just didn't have time. The next day she prepared a peanut-butter-and-jelly sandwich for him and put it in a little container in her mailbox. The postal worker left her a note thanking her and revealed that his wife was undergoing cancer treatment and this sandwich was exactly what she always made him. From that day forward, unless she was out of town, the woman left him a sandwich, until his wife got back on her feet. Neither one of them ever forgot the mailbox sandwiches, as the woman truly delivered a world of difference.

The thank-you cycle. When I was a youngster and my bicycle broke, we took it to Mr. Cohen, the bicycle man. He fixed my bike and it was like new. I drew a picture of him, accompanied by a poem that I wrote, and Mr. Cohen framed my letter and kept it in his store. Whenever we went back, I saw my thank-you proudly displayed on the wall. That image reminded me of how even at an early age, children can make a difference in someone's day and work life, and it boomerangs back to us, too. Involve your kids in perpetuating thanks throughout your lives. You're never too young or too old to say "thank you."

> **LOL:** Appreciation is a gift you can always give. It costs nothing and is easy to share. Involve everyone in your family or workplace in spreading gratitude. Kindness at work is contagious.

Volunteer and Give Back

Ken Byers is chairman of the Sandy Springs Arts Foundation, devoted to serving the arts communities and underserved causes, and he and his wife recently endowed a spectacular theater for a performing arts center. When I asked why he gives, he responded, "Because it feels damn good." Ken nailed it.

Whether you are a CEO like Ken, who has devoted his time and resources to making an impact on our community; an employee; or a volunteer, getting involved in civic-minded concerns feels amazing. No two people have the same kindness thumbprint on this earth. Finding what you or your family, colleagues, or company is passionate about reveals your unique thumbprint of caring. Together we can give back to a variety of causes, address community needs, and support others with our time.

Where Can You Volunteer Today?

It often takes time to match yourself with a cause that speaks to your heart, but when you find the right one, it's a remarkable way to love out loud. Here are some places to network and think about volunteering:

- **Community.** Think of timely needs your community has, from elections to hunger to organized events, like breast cancer walks to raise awareness and funds. Volunteer at the check-in table if you want to meet new people, and find a way to put your skills and talents to work. Brighten your backyard — your community — and open up your heart.

- **Schools.** Your nearby schools, or places where your children or other family went to school, welcome all help. Perhaps you can be a reader, or even a listener to children who need to read out loud for practice. There are endless ways our educational systems need support.

- **Neighborhoods.** Think about how you can beautify and improve your surrounding neighborhood or another neighborhood in need. From picking up trash to planting flowers, there are many ways to make a difference in your own backyard.

- **Nonprofit causes.** There are endless worthy causes in our world, both locally and nationally. Consider what you are passionate about, and get involved. From your local place of worship to a food bank or homeless shelter, find a way to connect with something that lifts another person in need.

- **Your religious organization.** If you belong to a house of worship, make an appointment to see the rabbi, priest, or religious leader. Ask how you can make a difference. Is there any way you can get involved, donating your time and talents, and give back?

> **LOL:** Giving feels "damn good." Do not postpone kindness.

Volunteer as a Company

Cheryl Kortemeier, executive director of the Corporate Volunteer Council of Atlanta, dedicated to civic engagement in the workplace, shared, "Kindness in the workplace goes a long way toward improving employee morale and may even create positive business results. Many employers offer opportunities for their employees to express kindness through serving others."

Cheryl highlighted two such opportunities:

When places of work create employee assistance programs or employee volunteer programs, employees have a chance to support their colleagues in times of need and to support their communities in meaningful ways. Employee assistance programs may allow coworkers to contribute dollars to support fellow employees during times of hardship, missed work, or financial need. Employee volunteer programs may offer workplace-sponsored volunteer opportunities where colleagues come together to effect meaningful, positive change in the community. Both programs allow individuals to express kindness to others while improving perceptions about their employers — a win-win for everyone.

Sensitivity training. Kindness at work can make a world of difference, even to the world of one person. Begin inside the culture of a company or volunteer organization by encouraging sensitivity to each other, caring, and recognition of the importance of each person's story and presence.

When Michael Greenbaum, a philanthropist and truly kindhearted man, established a nonprofit arm of his company called Tower Lights, he created a powerful mission dedicated to inspiring his employees to show up, helping a variety of underserved causes. Employees are invited to share causes they are passionate about, bringing in speakers from a variety of community nonprofits who need help, and they volunteer monthly.

Michael and his equally generous wife, Anne, are a special pair of good-hearted individuals who selflessly give their time, talents, and treasures at every possible opportunity. When Michael was asked why he gives, he responded, "When I see suffering, I have to do something." Michael's hope is to inspire his employees, friends, and family to join him and continue the giving by getting everyone involved. He created this company-wide volunteer program to support these efforts, and to date has helped raise awareness and over $2 million for worthwhile causes.

> **LOL:** Make it your business's business to give back and be helpful to your community. Do not miss an opportunity to give and inspire others to join you.

Give Awards and Recognition

Be a giver! I love to give company or community awards for a variety of reasons whenever possible. Trophies commemorating a living legend for a special birthday or a "PhD" in the field of caring or friendship is meaningful, especially when presented out loud at a company meeting, gathering, or event.

Seal it with praise. Linda, a dedicated veteran employee at a high-profile company, commented, "The best recognition I ever received was a letter written to me from the president on my birthday thanking me for the outstanding job I had done that year. His kind words, sincere praise, and specific details of how I was valued in the company were the most meaningful gift I could have gotten that day. Add to that the fact that he gave it to me in person on my birthday, and it truly left me speechless."

Give an "Iron Will Award." Be creative when giving an award, and honor an admirable trait in someone else.

Recently, I was reminded of the power of words when I was given a surprise Iron Will Award at the children's concert I oversee that benefits Children's Healthcare of Atlanta. While this honor was certainly lovely, it was what was written on the award — a note of thanks recognizing my persistence in not giving up working to raise awareness for the music therapy program and funds to support it — that made me feel as though my determined efforts were truly appreciated.

Mentoring and Employee Recognition

- **Be boss for the day.** Honor someone who is doing a great job by either trading places or making them boss for the day. Meet and discuss any specific things that need handling, but this is a wonderful honor for someone who shows promise and potential.

- **Reward the overtime bucket.** Have a weekly or monthly drawing where everyone who puts in overtime hours or does something kind adds their name to the bucket. Pull names at the end of the period, and award gift cards or even some time off.

- **Share the applause.** Give each employee two five-dollar gift cards for coffee or something nearby they'll enjoy. One is to enjoy themselves, and the other is to give away to another employee who does something kind.

- **Mentor an employee.** Select and recognize an employee in need or who is showing promise, and mentor them. Putting our stock in human potential is one of the most amazing investments that we can make in life and the strongest way to help someone grow at work. Teach another person how you do what you do, manage time, get organized, get to work on time, and succeed. Share the traits you value about yourself, and get to know the employee. Set goals and set a new path for their success.

- **Plan a thank-you meeting.** A woman who had been at a small company for fifteen years wanted to turn the office morale around and inspire everyone to be more positive. She called a VIP meeting and named it the thank-you meeting. Now, five years later, the company ends every staff meeting by going around the table with a goodwill comment.

Ideas for Celebrating Birthdays at Work

Everyone's birthday counts. Maintaining a list of birthdays can easily be managed by a Birthday Ambassador. Take the initiative to create a birthday tradition at your business, and have some sort of celebration, small or big, for everyone on their day.

- **Invite the birthday singers.** When it's someone's birthday, one office gathers everyone together in the lunchroom while the person is serenaded by the company singers (who are employees who love to sing). It's a little thing but alerts coworkers as to who is having a birthday, and birthday wishes follow all day. The company singers are also available to sing to customers, clients, and others by phone or in person at events and now have a medley of songs for every occasion.

- **Circulate a card for everyone to sign.** Sounds simple, but including coworkers in well wishes makes everyone feel good and spreads happiness. It's a special thing to know that everyone added their name to a card selected just for you.

- **Institute the birthday desk buddy.** One office has a statue (it could also be a stuffed toy or anything that's fun or symbolic of your company), and whenever it's someone's birthday, the office "Birthday Buddy" arrives on that individual's desk until it's the next person's birthday.

- **Celebrate birthdays with unique themes monthly.** Depending on the month, look up what special days are celebrated nationally and you'll discover a variety of creative themes, or invent your own. Incorporate those into a monthly birthday celebration. Have a pie day. Chocolate day. Cupcake day. Cookie day. Or a "We love you berry much" day with fresh fruit in season. This idea works well even in the absence of a birthday to liven up your office's morale with treats, sweets, and midday snacks.

One CEO arranged for everyone in the company to gather in the lobby of their office after lunch on the first workday of each month, and a cake arrived for the monthly birthdays. He also had an ice-cream truck outside. It was a monthly gathering to celebrate everyone and made the employees feel like kids again with their choice of ice-cold treats.

One company's employees show up in the hall at noon and sing "Happy Birthday" on people's birthdays. Occasionally they'll play disco music, and everyone has a ten-minute dance party. It might sound crazy, but talk about *fun*: this office has a blast, and even the most timid of employees has learned to join in.

> **LOL:** Never miss an opportunity to be proud out loud at work. Celebrate each person, team, or branch office even if only virtually, giving a shout-out for birthdays, special occasions, work anniversaries, and more.

A Memorable Retirement Celebration

When Dr. Peter Gordon retired from his ophthalmology practice after thirty-five years, his office organized a surprise retirement celebration in his honor. It was clearly an amazing display of affection at work. His coworkers invited his wife, Norma, and all his children and grandchildren. They also invited fifty-plus of his original nurses and staff members to attend.

Everyone paid him loving tributes, and one employee shared a story about how every day for three and a half decades, Dr. Gordon stopped by her desk to say good morning, ask how she was, and grab a package of peanut-butter crackers, which she had a stash of. She said how she loved his greetings but kiddingly also remarked that she was not sure if he really wanted to talk to her or get the crackers! She presented him with five cases of peanut-butter crackers as a farewell. The office also "retired" his internal physician provider number on a jersey as a send-off. It was mounted in a shadow-box frame and truly reflected the visible love everyone had for this doctor.

Kindness Works!

While this chapter celebrates putting kindness to work, the "love out loud" mission is alive and at work one day at a time. Our actions tap dozens of people daily, and a kind word can positively affect another's day, their job, and even their life. We can add miles of smiles to our work, whatever it is — be it volunteering, logging hours remotely, or staying home raising children.

There will be times when you spread love like wildfire, and others when *you* will be the one who needs the world to lift you up or give you a hand. Being a gracious receiver is as important as the role of the giver. Welcome the love when others share their genuine interest and concern for your well-being. If we all work at spreading kindness and let our kind hearts do the talking, we can truly build a better world.

LOL: At work and throughout your life, share good deeds, kind words, and thoughtful actions. Celebrating each other in purposeful and creative ways at work makes people feel cherished. Share a love for others everywhere you go with your signature touch.

Kindness works! When love goes to work, we employ kindness. Sign up and apply today!

Three LOL Things You Can Do Today at Work

1. **Get to know a coworker better every week.** Reach out today and take the time to make a connection with one coworker, colleague, or employee. Create a rapport that lets someone know they are important.

2. **Give sincere praise freely to others.** Show genuine gratitude to the individuals you work or volunteer with, and get to know their contributions. How do they make your workplace better? Noticing what others do right creates a spirit of teamwork. It helps to be surrounded by people you value and enjoy.

3. **Think of ways you can make your workplace or volunteer organization better because you are there.** Envision the outcome. Add your signature for success. It's a simple concept, but every day and in every way you can give thought to your possible impact and help contribute to a better, more efficient, earth-friendly work environment.

CHAPTER 8

CREATING LOVE-OUT-LOUD MOMENTS AND GIFTS

Special times shared and gifts that say "I love you," "You are valued," and "Thank you" are long remembered and treasured. These are tiny miraculous moments and little acts of kindness that make us feel cherished. Kind people don't just give a gift; they leave an imprint on our hearts. That's what this chapter is all about. These LOL moments and gifts are filled with kind intentions that speak loudly and clearly.

Spending time with someone — for example, gifting tickets to attend a concert together — can bring us closer than all the material gifts on earth. When someone seeks out our company, we feel that we matter to them, and it lets us know that we are valued, appreciated, even adored. These gifts, while invisible, are heartfelt. Others are more tangible. But all have the power to bring endless joy and touch us deeply.

The magical moments and gifts suggested in this chapter have a common thread: they share a language of loving out loud. It is in that consciousness, through the emotions evoked, we feel inspired and treasured. These gifted moments are locked and loaded in our hearts to cherish for years to come.

Gifts that connect us hold a deeper meaning and come in all shapes and sizes. Search for clues to better understand what someone truly values, and give in a way that shows how much you care: by loving out loud.

The Music of Love, Sweet Love

Music, with its ability to inspire and uplift, is an expressive way to love someone out loud, especially when you know the genre they love most and listen to a song's meaning. Whether you share a special song for your first dance at your wedding, or you have a theme song yourself that motivates and inspires you, there are many ways music can touch you and remind you to love out loud.

Since this book's goal is to spread love, in the hopes of helping make the world a better place, my remarkably caring friend Tena Clark — an award-winning

music producer, composer, lyricist, and author —
shared her thoughts about the 1960s hit "What the
World Needs Now Is Love" (lyrics by Hal David, music
composed by Burt Bacharach, and recorded by Dionne
Warwick) and the writer behind it:

> Hal David was a huge inspiration in my career.
> He gave me his attention and guidance when
> I was just a kid, living on a farm in rural Mis-
> sissippi. Hal was a mentor to me until the end
> of his life. He believed in me. When someone
> believes in you, it's contagious — you must pay
> it forward.
>
> In my life and career, music equals love.
> It's a language. It's a teacher. Music is an emo-
> tional connector for all of us. Music transcends
> all boundaries, walls, and religions. Dionne
> Warwick had it right when she sang that time-
> less song. It is as relevant today as it was over
> fifty years ago. I believe love is the only law we
> need. Love can and will heal this world. With-
> out love why are we here? We are sisters, we are
> brothers, we are all God's children.

In the spirit of love, every day we have opportunities all around us. Our family, friends, and teachers love
us out loud, for they inspire us to get in touch with our
abilities and acknowledge our potential. How do you
spread love? My husband adores classical music, which

he finds relaxing, and every day he has a symphony, concerto, or overture playing. He loves sharing it and getting others excited about his musical preferences.

When you tune in to the language of love through music or any of your interests or talents, you open yourself up to a richer and more rewarding present. Music is indeed a labor of love, and we all become teachers when we share our love of music out loud.

Dr. Warren Woodruff — classical musicologist and pianist, educator, writer, and creator of Dr. Fuddle, a classical music educational mission for children — underscored the importance of teaching:

> Teaching another human being the artful craft of music making is truly an act of kindness. For with that passing of knowledge, one is passing many great gifts and treasures that will endure throughout a lifetime. What greater demonstration of kindness could there be than taking extra time of one's own to endow another with a sense of accomplishment...than providing inspiration that will last a lifetime? What could be kinder than patiently going that extra mile to help a child know that they can do something special if they only put their mind to it and devote their heart and soul to making it happen? Teaching music provides a sense of gratification like few other professions can in life; and in so doing we, as musicians

and teachers, are also passing love, joy, passion, and a gift that keeps on giving forever.

> **LOL:** The language of love has no limits and knows no bounds, and these magical moments that truly touch our hearts and souls are where loving out loud lives and breathes.

Focus on the Manner in Which You Gift

As a nationally known gift-giving expert, I have reported for over three decades on this art. I'm still surprised by how the smallest of gifts or deeds, or just a few written words, can have an impact on someone's entire life. I have learned from thousands of gift givers and recipients what truly touches them, and which gifts and sentiments have ultimately been the most treasured of all. I have also learned that individuals' likes and wants change. One year gift cards nail it, while the next year the soundtrack to a hot Broadway play hits the sweet spot.

To become a gift-giving pro…

- **Pay attention.** You, too, can be a pro at this endeavor. Instead of thinking of it as a material exchange, look upon it as a wonderful way to give someone your attention. Gift giving is a language unto itself. When you notice what another person values, appreciates, and enjoys; their likes and dislikes; their passions and preferences, you are paying attention. That attention, when gifted, is interpreted as caring and validation. The recipient feels you know them. Where does he shop? Where does she go to get her nails done? What's his favorite restaurant? What causes does he support, and would a donation in his honor be meaningful? Get the details. When you give a gift that truly reflects the recipient, you are caring out loud. A perfect present becomes a memory refresher, reminding the recipient of your kindness and love that came with the gift.

- **Consider how your gift is presented.** Think about how your gift is delivered. From incorporating the element of surprise to wrapping the gift with love, take the time to make it memorable. Remember, a gift makes a first impression, even before it's opened or enjoyed. Talk to friends and family about the best gift they've ever been given, and keep a record. Prepare for gift giving, and add your personal signature flair. Stock up on gifts that you adore, from your favorite books to a candy that's a home-run hit. Have personalized stickers and wrapping paper on hand to dress up even the simplest of gifts. If you have children, involve them in creating the gift wrap, as their artistic talents hand-printing craft paper or including artwork are to be treasured.

- **Remember, some gifts are invisible.** When we help a friend's child by writing a letter of recommendation, shop for someone who is infirm, give a donation to support a cause anonymously, or mentor someone in need, we are loving out loud. Or would a friend value your time and talents helping her get organized or learn to cook a special dish? These are the gifts you *can't* wear, and one size does not fit all. Knowing that you made a difference in someone else's life is the gift to top all gifts. Be generous with your time, talents, and treasures, and look for opportunities behind the scenes to share the gifts of your spirit.

- **Give out of a spirit of generosity.** While we were traveling through Australia, a woman offered to help our friends with their luggage. This stranger went out of her way to help the couple manage the baggage they were trying to check on the plane. Amid the long lines and obvious travel challenges, this total stranger saved them a lot of grief while navigating what could be carried on board. In awe of her actions, I asked the woman, who was standing behind me, what inspired her to help, and she said, "Aussies step up. We do the right thing. We've all experienced a time when we needed help, and coming to someone's rescue is important. It's the right thing to do." Always remember that gifts that come from the heart *enter* the heart.

How to creatively give LOL gifts

- **Make the delivery special.** The manner in which you give the gift can be a fun experience itself.

Tie a ball of yarn or a string to a gift, and put the unraveled end by someone's nightstand. Add the note "Follow me and a gift you'll see." Unwind the string all over the house with your gift at the end of it. The gift could be a love letter, a special treat you baked, or even an IOU for ten hugs.

- **Make it picture-perfect.** Create a slideshow or share photographs that capture love. It's easy to take snapshots at someone's special event — a birthday party, wedding, or baby naming — and include lots of little details capturing special family members' expressions and moments that are price-less. Learn how to create the slideshow quickly with an app, and add music. I often gift it immediately following the event as a token of thanks. I enjoy the experience and love to capture their moments in a personalized movie. A beautiful framed photo montage was a picture-perfect gift of gratitude I received from Lynn Stallings, executive director of Atlanta Workshop Players, following an event that I worked on. It was a special keepsake photo show-casing the talented kids who performed in this meaningful benefit concert.

   Christine Pullara also described a favorite gift: "I have the pleasure of working with someone who's become a dear friend, Cara Kneer. We take pictures together all the time in our line of work, and one day after a particularly challenging day we took a silly picture of us both looking exasperated.

For Christmas last year she made it into an ornament! I leave it out all year long, and it makes me laugh every time I see it. It reminds me, 'No matter how tough things get, remember you are loved and there's always tomorrow!'"

- **Gift a gathering of friends.** It's always so special to get a group of friends together to celebrate a birthday, the recovery from an illness, an engagement, a new baby on the way, or anything else of importance. Surprise your friend and let everyone contribute one dish, a toast, or a poem about the person. Issue the guest of honor the invite to attend from "secret admirers" to add a little intrigue, and be the one to drive to wherever everyone meets so your friend will know it's the real deal.

- **Give a box of wishes.** When a dear friend's son was diagnosed with cancer, everyone wanted to send him a get-well wish, so I began a box collecting the cards from friends, plus famous people, athletes, and anyone I ran into who'd sign a get-well card to him. The box was soon filled with hundreds of cards, and we decorated it with his favorite football team's colors. The abundance of love he received cheered him up. I'm grateful to say he's in remission, and he mentions the cards every time he sees me.

- **Send a one-a-day "get well soon."** My friend Bettye sent her family member who was ill a card every day until she got well. She loaded up on cards with inspirational quotes and mailed them daily, determined to cheer her up. Add a note that says: "Until you're feeling swell — these cards will wish you well." And when her brother in another city was having a big birthday, she also sent seventy cards in a box. Yes, it was wild, but Bettye said he laughed and read every single one and loved her birthday wishes.

- **Give voices of love.** If you wish to send get-well thoughts to someone who is in another city or too ill to have company, write a beautiful letter to be read out loud. Share fond memories and stories that remind someone how much they are loved by you. Ask the caregiver or a family member to read the letter on your behalf. When my friend's dad was in hospice, I found a company that would let everyone call in their messages, and they were preserved in a music-style box. It meant so much to him and the entire family to hear everyone's sweet messages each time the box was opened. We all couldn't come see him due to a limit on visitors, but he still heard everyone's voice and listened repeatedly to their loving wishes.

- **Just name it!** A mother-in-law wanted to gift her adult kids something not material since she felt they really didn't need anything. She had a designer create a family emblem and printed the logo on T-shirts. The emblem was like a modern-day coat of arms for her surname, and everyone adores

using it on everything from stationery to family reunion signs.

- **Offer the gift of choice.** Don't know what to give
someone? For one of my friends who seems to
have everything, I preselected three gifts I thought
she'd like at the mall and took her to visit all three.
One of the items was a big hit. She'll never forget
my treasure hunt for her gift and loved being able
to pick out what she wanted.

- **Give a "standing" ovation.** A gift of appreciation
that Bill Savitt, the beloved business leader devoted to P.O.M.G. ("Peace of mind guaranteed")
service, received decades ago is now treasured by
his daughter, Spring. It is a carved statue of a man
doing a handstand demonstrating how "he bends
over backward and would stand on his head" to
serve his customers.

- **Make it homemade or handmade.** A crocheted
sweater or scarf, a workshop creation in wood, or
something else homemade and handmade is a gift
that adds your touch and includes a piece of you in
it that says "I love you." A photograph you take on
a special day or with a meaningful story attached is
also a beautiful gift. My son snapped a photo of a
butterfly while vacationing with Grandma Phyllis
at the beach. It hung in her home for many years
and reminded us of seaside times shared.

- **Gift a song rewrite.** Be creative and rewrite the
lyrics to a well-known song to make it all about

someone who is celebrating a birthday or special occasion. Perform the song at a party, luncheon, or event. Add relevant props, plus lots of love, and watch how much enjoyment singing your wishes and sentiments out loud can bring, even if you're an amateur singer. Provide the lyrics to the guest of honor, as your sweet melody will be music to their ears for years to come.

> **LOL:** Add a purpose and your presence to your present. Consider those you care about, and start a list of what they love — from their favorite cookie, type of chocolate, ice-cream flavor, or genre of book to a worthy cause they care about. Take notes and keep a record of these details. When it's gift time, give something that shows you noticed their preferences and personality characteristics, and be creative in your delivery.

Incredible and Edible Gifts

You don't have to be a foodie to appreciate a great meal. Everyone loves good food, especially their favorite type, dishes, or recipes. There are many clever gourmet ways to celebrate LOL moments, and here are some:

Have a recipe-exchange and tasting party. Invite twelve friends to bring a dozen copies of a favorite recipe, along with a dozen "tastes" if possible, and each share how they made their delight. Everyone leaves with each other's recipes and a little treat.

Create a freezer-pleaser party. Get six friends together who love to cook, bake, or even make winter warm-up soup. Everyone attends the party with six freezer-size name- and date-marked containers to feed two people each. You not only leave with the recipe for making it, but also 6 containers to stock your freezer. It's a fun party with a super-soup fabulous theme.

Throw an LOL dinner party. One of my favorite dinner parties was a New Year's Eve celebration where I collaged place cards with details that identified each guest. If he loved tennis, then a little tennis racket was glued to the card, along with other images ranging from his favorite sports team or color to the type of pet he owned. Each guest had to find their seat at the dining-room table with the card that clearly was meant for them. During the meal we went around the table and each shared a story about the details on the place card. It ignited an engaging conversation and made each guest feel special. Another idea I enjoy is writing a little poem on each place card such as: "Arlene's amazing and Marshall's our pal / When it comes to being wonderful, the Hoffmans know how!"

Give a potluck party. It's a tried-and-true idea: a potluck party lets everyone contribute something that they'd like to bring to the meal. Select a specific theme, such as Italian or comfort food. Volunteer to make the main dish if that's your specialty, and invite everyone else to bring the sides.

Design a food tour. Take your bestie or a family member who loves food out for an afternoon of food tastings. Arrange ahead of time for little samples or tastes at each of the destinations, and meet the chef, owners, or staff who can bring their food outlet to life. If your friend is a vegan or gluten-free eater or has special preferences, focus on food they can enjoy most. Purchase gift cards at a few of their favorite places so they can return and enjoy more.

Gift a dinner on you. Television emcee and radio personality Tom Sullivan gave me a gift card to a popular restaurant chain to thank me for my support and longtime friendship. It was of course unnecessary, as I adore Tom and he's such a professional at everything he does, but he made me feel so appreciated. My husband and I enjoyed a delicious dinner, compliments of Tom. What I truly treasured was the fact that he also called and personally shared why he gave it: to thank me for being his friend. I could sense the sincerity in his heart, and it meant a great deal to me to hear how important it was to Tom to share his gratitude. I call that being an "emcee of kindness."

Collect food for those in need. Add an element of caring to your next party, birthday, or other special occasion. Ask everyone to bring a bag of canned foods or items with a long shelf life for a shelter or food bank. Show your gratitude for the food on your table by ensuring that someone else is fed. Add a blessing to everything you do, and spread the giving.

> **LOL:** Instead of just giving a dinner party, throw a dinner party or luncheon *with a purpose* to honor a friend's accomplishment, a new baby, becoming a grandparent, or a recent engagement or family member's wedding.

Gifts That Go Back in Time

Time is a gift unto itself. Think of ways to re-create a memory from the past, and involve the senses with experiential things to see, hear, smell, taste, and touch. When you bring to life something familiar (or otherwise) that elicits beautiful shared memories, you are giving a loving gift of the senses that neither you nor the recipient will ever forget.

Deliver a blast from the past. Take a friend back to your old neighborhood where you both grew up, or visit, if possible, some of their old favorite places to shop or play. When the fair returned to my hometown, I went with my childhood friend Linda, just like we used to do when we were in elementary school. We had a blast, with nonstop laughter, cotton candy, and more.

Let the music do the talking. Think of the music you listened to when you were sixteen. In all likelihood, you'll remember the words to most songs by favorite musicians during that era. Music is one of the last things to leave our memory and is a universal way to love someone out loud. Send a song via YouTube or give a CD of oldies. Or utilize a song's message to share your feelings. Tell her she's "My Girl," or tell him he's "Unforgettable." Let your daughter know she is "Beautiful," or lift up someone's spirits with "Happy." It's easy to select music or search for "golden oldie" concerts if you wish to gift an LOL experience.

Picture this. If you have a treasured personal, non-copyrighted photograph of a special event from the past, a beloved family member, or a time you shared with someone you care about, have it transformed into a gift. These days you can have almost anything done that makes it memorable. From mugs to charms to keychains, consider a way to give a picture-perfect gift that reminds the recipient they are picture-perfect.

Seal it with a kiss. I inherited a dozen new lipsticks when my mom, of blessed memory, passed away. She stocked up on a specific brand and color red, just in case it was discontinued. I framed one of the lipsticks and put it away and donated the others to a good cause. Before you discard your loved ones' possessions, think about the items that have deeper meaning. For me, it was a kiss from my mom, and the lipstick said it all.

Forget me not. Following their mother's passing, my editor's family gathered a box of her mementos, including little statues, pretty plates, and vases, and gave it to the manager of the building where she had lived for other residents to choose from. It was a special way to honor their mother, and the residents appreciated this kind gesture done in her memory.

Have a dine-around dinner. Go to a few of your favorite restaurants, having an appetizer at one, a meal at another, and then dessert at a third. If you do this with a group, everyone could choose a different restaurant and make the arrangements. Choose comfort-food picks especially, or restaurants from your childhood if they are still in business. Ask everyone to be prepared to share memories and music from back in the day, throw-back facts, and TV trivia from way back when.

Leave a heartfelt message. My friend Jessica shared that she saved my message that I left on her phone since I could not reach her, and she found it comforting. Her husband had been diagnosed with cancer, and while I wanted to speak to her, not her voice mail, I did not want to delay my love: "Jessica, I just heard Danny was facing an illness, and I want you to know I love you both and am here for you. I will continue to call to check on you. Please do not be concerned about calling me back. It's my turn to reach out to you, and I am thinking of you nonstop." I have learned that our voice is a powerful thing, so before you speak, consider what you want to say and leave an inspiring message.

Traditions for Every Season

Throughout the year, there are endless ways to celebrate each other, our relationships, and moments in time through honoring traditions from the past or creating new ones. Here are some that have stood out as truly loving out loud:

Seasonal foods. Perhaps there is a family member who loved a specific food. As I mentioned in chapter 2, when peaches are in season, my husband waits until the ripest ones are available at the farmers market, and he purchases baskets of them. He puts a few in recycled bags and drops them off to friends, family, and neighbors. It's his way of loving others by sharing what he loves. He prides himself on ensuring the peaches are at their very best, for a peach-perfect experience.

Valentine's Day. The spirit of Valentine's Day can be alive year-round, but on that special day, it's about spreading love and expressing it out loud. Hide Post-it notes with loving words in your significant other's pockets, briefcase, lunch, or car — or anywhere they'll discover the love notes over time. Purchase kids' valentines and send a friend an envelope filled with them. Share Valentine's candy with the LOL note that says, "A little treat because you're so sweet." Or do something nice for someone who'll never know *you* were responsible. Donate to a cause or sponsor a kid's month of lunches at a local school. Pay for the person behind you at a parking lot, or treat someone to a cup of coffee or a meal by informing the server of your intentions. That's selfless giving, and you'll receive so much in return knowing you brightened someone's Valentine's.

When it comes to your significant other, consider gifting a year of "I love you's" said out loud, one a day. Your valentine will never tire of hearing your kind, sincere, and loving words.

Mother's Day. One family has a yearly omelet-brunch tradition every Mother's Day and decorates the table with photographs of beloved moms, past and present. Every year following the festive meal, they give their mom a perfect day filled with her favorite things to do, including a family walk in the park. Mother's Day is an occasion to truly say "Thank you, Mom" (or your grandmother, your aunt, or someone who has been like a mom to you). If Mom loves nature, have everyone bring a plant to the brunch, and let all the kids help plant their love out loud.

Father's Day. A father of three boys shared with me how his father wrote him a letter with little lessons every Father's Day. He saved all the letters in a beautiful box and continued the tradition, writing each of his sons a letter on Father's Day. Now his boys are fathers, and the tradition lives on. The sons all get together and share memories from their dad's letters, and they treasure the ones their grandfather wrote their father. Every year this priceless paternal wisdom is handed down.

Independence Day. Call your local VA hospital and veterans' causes to see how you can brighten the lives of those who have served their country. Donating items to those in need is just one way to show your support for troops and veterans. Volunteering on July 4 is a wonderful way to add meaning to the holiday that celebrates our independence and freedom. Be proud out loud of your servicemen and women.

Back to school. Take a photo of your kids with a sign that states the grade they are in that year. You'll treasure the photographs and always know the child's age in each. Every year put the photo away so that when a child comes of age, you have already assembled the most amazing gift of photographs over the years.

Halloween. A family with four children who loved to trick-or-treat shared their yearly "trick-or-treat — let's be sweet" family Halloween tradition. The kids traded in all the candy collected, except enough for one week, for coupons that replaced all the sugar with books, experiences at the park, and eating-out gift cards. They then took the candy to a good cause that was collecting it for a holiday party. They also packaged small gift-size bags and delivered them to nursing homes while wearing Halloween costumes (which they and everyone there loved).

Sweet sixteen. On my daughter's sixteenth birthday, we crafted a treasure hunt that took her to sixteen memorable sights in New York City. Instead of being spelled out on an itinerary, every outing had a clue she'd read out loud, so the treasure hunt led us around the Big Apple for a whirlwind weekend filled with excitement. From frozen hot chocolate at Serendipity 3 to a visit to the Statue of Liberty, her sixteenth birthday was big on fun and became a lasting memory.

Anniversary of your sweet-sixteen birthday. This works for the anniversary of any later year that's celebrated, such as your twenty-fifth year since your sweet sixteen, which makes you forty-one. Childhood friends of mine gave a fiftieth anniversary of their sweet-sixteen party, since all the friends, now sixty-six, had thrown a joint party when they turned sixteen. There are many ways to spin this idea, including the twenty-fifth anniversary party of your twenty-first birthday (at age forty-six).

Half birthday. If you want a creative way to celebrate someone whose birthday is months away, focus on their half birthday. Kids especially love this. Throw a "half-birthday party," serve half a cake, and enjoy this halfway version of a celebration.

Bridal shower. If you want to love the bride out loud, consider a gift of something blue, new, or old, as in a vintage gift. One mother gifted her daughter her mother's beautiful linens and a set of sterling silver.

Most brides want gifts from their bridal registries, so also consider giving the gift of choice and sticking to the tried-and-true. Add a poem, a fun toast, or a meaningful message that relates to the gift. Or gift a gift card to a popular restaurant for a future date night out.

Baby shower. Oh baby! Show your love for that bundle of joy to come by creating a theme that celebrates the new arrival. From "Twinkle, Twinkle, Little Star" to "Think Pink" or "Oh Boy!" — the sky's the limit. A fun game to play is letting everyone guess the date and time of the baby's birth, and whoever is right wins a special prize. Save the guesses and announce the winner when the baby is born. Gifts for a new baby include an "I love you" library of books about love, or a "good night" selection that puts baby or a toddler to sleep. Add a disclaimer poem to be read aloud, just in case they don't work: "These books are yours to read and keep / *Hopefully*, they will help put your baby to sleep."

Bar or Bat Mitzvah. A grandmother named SuSu gave her grandson the gift of choice as he celebrated his Bar Mitzvah, becoming a man at the age of thirteen. Taking him to shop for the watch of his choice, she reminded him how much she loves spending time with him, and the gift became symbolic of that. Occasionally, she will text him asking him the time. The time spent together was the best gift of all.

Wedding. On the wedding day, a groom had a love letter delivered on a silver platter to his bride professing his promise of love to her. Another bride had an engraved watch delivered to her partner on the rooftop garden of the hotel where they were getting married, and she shared how she was looking forward to the time of her life and spending it together. The watch was engraved with the letters *ILYM*, which stood for "I love you more."

Second marriage. When gifting a second marriage, find out if the couple has a cause they care about, and donate to it. Ask the couple what would be most meaningful to them, as some have registered for gifts or worthy causes and others have not. Or give stationery, gift-enclosure cards, or something that is useful personalized with their new names or initials. Personalized luggage tags are also popular for the couple on the go. A favorite gift for garden lovers was a gift card to the local plant nursery, cooking classes went to the foodie newlyweds, while another couple who traveled nonstop was given a group gift of matching carry-on lightweight luggage.

Gift a Forget-Me-Not Collection

In the over three decades I have reported on the topic of giving, I have moved from focusing on the material objects we gift each other (which, certainly, we all appreciate) to the things that endure through the ages. I have taken note of gifts that become people's most precious, beloved treasures.

When gifting love-out-loud gifts, consider these points:

- Think about a feeling and message you wish your gift to convey. The recipient will remember how you made them feel above anything else. Make them feel loved.
- Gift something that is timeless, memorable, and lasting and will be easy to store, move, and save over time.
- Gift something that leaves behind a symbol of what you stand for, a value, a personality trait you wish to be remembered by, or how you feel about the recipient.

Some collections to gift

- **A novel idea.** Lisa, a former teacher, gave her grandchildren bookends, and each birthday, she gives a new book that is printed and released in the same year. As time goes by, she hopes to build a beautiful collection of beloved books that celebrate each year of their lives with love from her.
- **Dreidel time.** Patty started a dreidel collection for her daughter and now gifts one each Hanukkah to her grandchildren. Each child gets a unique dreidel

that she finds during the holiday. Its symbolism is based on her love for each of them.

- **Game on.** I admire the marble collection a grandfather inherited from his grandfather. He continues to search for beautiful additions to this tiny collection that he loves, and he teaches all the children in the family the age-old game of marbles. He's also teaching them chess and checkers. The kids love to play with Grandpa.

- **A special spot in my heart.** My mother really didn't collect anything, but she did have a love for dalmatians. As I mentioned in chapter 6, for over thirty years, she and I went to Scott Market, a monthly antique market, searching for china dalmatians. I would often buy Staffordshire black-and-white spotted dogs and china from every imaginable era and tell her they just cost a few dollars, though they were quite valuable, to ensure she would accept my gift. We kept all the dogs at her home, and they filled a curio cabinet to the brim. I never wanted to become the dogs' owner, as I knew that would mean my mother would be gone. At the age of eighty-seven, she passed away and I did inherit the collection, which is one of my most prized. Not just because it's lovely to look at and reminds me of my dalmatians growing up, but because each dog represents times shared with my adored mother.

- **An artful gift.** A talented salon owner named Erik shared his favorite gift that truly made him feel loved: "For my birthday, my partner, Bryan, gave me a signed Matisse lithograph, and I was absolutely astounded. Every time I arrive home, I see it and it reminds me how much I am loved. Bryan is an interior designer, and he has also educated me about quality and beautiful things. He has increased my knowledge of collecting and taught me so much about beautiful interiors."

> **LOL:** When starting a collection for yourself or anyone you love, consider what it represents. Beyond the investment, one day what will it mean? Share your enthusiasm about it with friends and family, including grandchildren, while you are alive so that when it's time to pass it on, it has deeper meaning and history.

Gifts That Keep on Giving

There are many gifts that keep on giving, and hopefully this chapter will help you zoom in on them. Throughout our lives, we evolve and learn to let go of things — including gifts — that once closely defined us. Here are a few ways gift givers have embodied giving enduring, forever gifts:

- **Gift an heirloom you treasure today.** Don't wait until you are gone to pass on that special piece of jewelry or a priceless object handed down to you. Gift it with the story that the gift embodies so it has lasting meaning. Seeing someone enjoy the gift while you are alive is a gift itself.

- **Commemorate big birthdays with meaningful messages.** Whether it's to celebrate sweet sixteen, twenty-one, or the big five-oh, gift something that will always be associated with that birthday. Often a long-desired watch, which symbolizes the time you spend together, or twenty-one reasons why you love someone calligraphed in beautiful lettering can be a treasure. Gift a memory that makes someone feel loved far, far beyond measure.

- **Give "gifts on the go."** Plan a road trip. A pair of brothers get together every five years on their dad's big birthday and take him on a road trip. They plan the trip, which might include visiting everything from the Baseball Hall of Fame to famous barbecue restaurants; book Dad's ticket; and have a blast. They all look forward to their dad's birthday, and they talk about how much fun they all had for years after.

- **Make it memorable!** For my father's ninetieth birthday, our family stayed at a vacation house on the beach. Since my dad did not want any gifts, I hid ninety one-dollar bills all around the house, from inside clothing pockets to under placemats at the dinner table. All the kids (and adults) loved discovering the bills. At first my father thought the money belonged to the homeowner (my aunt and uncle) and should be returned. However, we lovingly shared how this treasure hunt was in his honor, because we treasure him! Everyone enjoyed finding the money, and we contributed it to charity in my dad's honor, which made it all the better.

- **Utilize the power of photography and online apps.** I enjoy creatively using technology. Whenever there's a special occasion or time shared, I photo-journal it by snapping pictures. My friend Gail brought over her precious two-year-old granddaughter, Zoey, and from the moment she arrived to the final bye-bye, I took pictures. I then used an app on my cell phone that in minutes allows me to make a slideshow to music, and a few hours after Gail had left, I sent it to her. It was a "virtual" keepsake that Gail shared with her entire family.

- **Don't give up!** When my son Justin called me to tell me I should listen to Coach Jimmy Valvano's unforgettable speech that he gave at the ESPY Awards on March 4, 1993, before he lost his life to cancer, I was so inspired and moved. Justin and I joined forces with the V Foundation and coauthored a book based on Jimmy V.'s famous speech called *Don't Give Up...Don't Ever Give Up*. There are so many inspiring stories, life-changing lectures, and life-affirming speeches and talks that are accessible online; check them out.

While I am very selective about what I share online, particularly through social media, I think about what might cause a ripple of change or love. Sometimes a sentimental post reminds me to be a little kinder or pay closer attention to those individuals I care about, as well as people I do not know.

> **LOL:** Consider a gift as an opportunity to create a lasting memory that will never fade. A memory is a precious keepsake that touches you and lives inside your heart.

Three LOL Things You Can Do Today to Give

1. **Gift experiences.** Remember that your time is one of the most powerful gifts you can give. Plan a picnic, a trip to the library, or another activity that you do together. "Together" gifts are long remembered.

2. **Add a little piece of yourself to every gift.** When you give a gift, consider the manner in which you give it, from the wrapping, presentation, words that accompany it, and what the gift says. A loving-out-loud gift speaks for itself. It says "Thank you, I love you, and you're special." Consider the next gift you have to give, and plan ahead and gift it with love.

3. **Remember, loving out loud *is* a gift.** That's right, and there are endless ways to give LOL gifts, from giving away an abundance of hugs; to making a personal call wishing someone a happy birthday; to sharing something you cherish, be it your mother's handkerchief, a trinket from your childhood, or a photo from the past. Transform someone's day: look them in the eye and smile. Share the love in your heart, and gift it generously.

CHAPTER 9

CHERISHING LOVED ONES AND PRESERVING MEMORIES

We inherit many things — from stories to memories and often even material possessions — from other generations. Understanding our loved ones' lives and embracing what really matters helps us preserve their legacies. These things hold powerful meaning, and when we care for them, cherished memories of loved ones linger on and can even be passed down.

Savor loving reminders of those special people you treasure. By doing so, you continue to tell the story of those individuals who have filled your life with love.

You can discover what speaks to you and serves to keep their voices and spirits alive.

Loving out loud is all about creating more meaning in your life: not collecting more material objects or amassing too much stuff, but rather learning to view as important the things and memories that keep you connected — to people you love, places you've been, and times you've shared. This consciousness of what matters truly contributes to a life well lived. Make a conscious effort to edit your life, winnowing it down to include what matters to you most. The goal is to surround yourself with the beauty of remembrances of those individuals in life who gave you love and immeasurable joy.

Some of these memories reflect special times in your life — for example, celebrating the birth of a child — or a treasured friendship or, sadly, friends and family who have passed. Though loved ones may have physically left us, their spiritual presence is all around us.

Value the Sentimental Connection

If I could give you one gift today, it would be the time to understand what your loved ones closest to you value and why. Before my mother passed away, I would ask her to tell me more and more about what she valued and all about some of her prized possessions. I learned bits and pieces over the years. When, sadly, it was apparent that her days were numbered, it was too late to ask all the remaining questions. I knew my mom loved a little pair of china figures she kept on her armoire, but to this day I have no idea where they came from. I can't part with them, recalling how they touched her. When I look at them, I think of her with love.

So how do you get in touch with true sentiment? Here are some questions to ask yourself and ways to connect:

- **What's the story?** Ask if a material possession has a personal story attached. Make notes for your family about things that mean a lot to you. Over the years, my mother frequently pointed out a small blue pitcher that was her grandmother's. I have the little blue bottle, and it reminds me of the amazing women before me.
- **What's the origin?** Find out where or whom an object came from. Not only does the provenance of many items add monetary value, but knowing where an object was purchased often tells you a great deal about it. Secure the story and find out the details. Was it brought from another country? Was it handed down from generation to generation?
- **Is it an heirloom?** If you inherit the gift of an heirloom, write down who owned it and on what occasion they received it or how old it might be. Over seventy-five years ago, one gentleman gifted his wife a diamond bar pin from Tiffany, a beautiful sun bursting with rays. Presented on the occasion of her giving birth to a son, it held very special meaning that made it priceless. That story

was passed down through the generations, and the pin shined with such a truly dazzling history. Sometimes, you can also find a photograph that includes the piece of jewelry being worn or an object you've inherited in the room. I recently located a photograph of my grandmother Annie with her sisters that was decades old. In the background was a bookshelf that held a photograph I now own of me as a baby. Talk about picture-perfect.

> **LOL:** Focus on a few possessions, and record or write down what each item means to you. Ensure their lasting loving value to future generations who will want to know to whom they belonged.

Treasuring Loving Reminders

Living with reminders of loved ones around us transforms our decor into a treasure chest of memories. I'm always touched when friends or family members find ways to celebrate loved ones and special times shared. For example, a sentimental daughter-in-law named Patty, who never had the chance to meet her father-in-law, as he passed way before she met her husband, framed his bow ties, a reminder of what a gentleman she'd heard he always was to everyone who knew him.

Here are some of the ideas I have implemented that continue to mean a great deal to me:

Pay attention when cleaning out a loved one's home. Every detail you find is potentially important. Open up boxes and books, and don't miss the little opportunities to connect with your loved one's life. A telephone number was sitting by my mother's desk after she passed away. I called it and when I said who I was, the woman who answered immediately identified herself and shared how my father and her husband (who had recently passed away) had been in the war together. She tearfully added, "Sweetheart, your father saved my husband." My modest father had never mentioned this, and that call meant the world to me.

Create a memory box. When my daughter Ali was born, I found a vintage heart-shaped box that had once held a sweetheart pattern of silverware. I lined it with satin and named it "Ali's Memory Box." The box held her baby shoes, her rattle, and a small assortment of other things from when she was just an infant, including her hospital baby bracelet and first curl. To this day this box brings back precious memories of the very precious time in my life when she was born.

Preserve heirlooms in a shadow box. Think of heirlooms that truly touch you. For example, if you have adult children, often when the kids move out of your house you are left with the yearbooks, photo albums, and objects from their childhood. Following the death of my mother, I discovered a metal storage box my mom had kept for years that contained the dress I had worn as a baby. I had the dress preserved and framed, and when my daughter was a baby, I saved her dress as well and had it framed. Today the shadow boxes of the baby dresses hang side by side along with a pair of photographs of myself and my daughter wearing them as infants.

Display medals to treasure. When my father passed, I discovered a box of his medals from his days in the naval air force, as he had been a blimp pilot in World War II. I had the medals framed with a photograph of my mother and him when they were engaged. I look at them often and wish I could sit down and talk to him more about his war experiences.

Create a video history. If you do one thing regarding your personal and family history, it ought to be to record an interview with a family member talking about the good old days. Take time now to glean information from family members who hold a window onto your past and knowledge of your family lore. Here are some conversation starters to get the person talking:

- "Do you recall any special memories about the day your children were born?"
- "What was going on in the world then?"
- "What are your earliest childhood memories?"
- "Who were your childhood friends?"
- "What was it like growing up where you did and being a teenager?"

- "What kind of music did you listen to?"
- "Do you remember your room or toys you played with as a child?"
- "What can you tell me about your parents and where they came from?"
- "What do you want me to share about them with future generations?"

> **LOL:** Ask the questions today you might regret not asking if you do not have the chance tomorrow. Do not delay, and preserve these memories. These conversations, video recorded or taped and transcribed, will ultimately be the greatest gift you'll ever give yourself.

Honor Loved Ones and the Dearly Departed

Loving out loud does not end with death. When someone is alive, they pour love into us. That love continues on as we pour it into others. As I have mourned loved ones in my life, I think of ways to keep their spirits and lessons they taught me alive. Another daughter went on a journey to her mother's hometown to walk in her childhood footsteps. She visited meaningful landmarks and viewed places through her mother's eyes from the stories she heard while growing up.

Volunteering or donating your time, treasures, or talents in memory of a loved one is a meaningful way to honor their life and add purpose to yours. Consider what is important to someone who has passed, and continue the action, good deed, or project they began. One family whose mother valued education now sponsors a yearly community-wide lecture in her memory and gives a scholarship in her name to a deserving outstanding student.

LOL Snapshot

Jan Collins, a community leader and volunteer who is a reservoir of kindness, always giving to others, shared a poignant story of a friend who inspired her: "When my friend Julie's husband died, she asked us all to do a week's worth of kindness in lieu of donations in her husband's memory." Wishing to honor that beautiful request, Jan picked up trash on her daily walks, weeded the cul-de-sac in her neighborhood, and then went to the grocery store and gave out five-dollar bills, thanking the employees who worked there. The grocery staff was surprised she wanted nothing in return, just to thank each of them, and they were so touched by this act of kindness.

> **LOL:** When someone passes away, consider what you might do to perpetuate their generous spirit that will make a difference in the lives of both the giver and the receiver.

You can love others out loud in myriad ways. Here are some heartwarming actions that keep the giving going:

Repurpose special clothing. Everyone referred to my father as "Honey" since that's what my mom called him over the years. As I cleaned out his closet after he died, it was like a time warp, with neatly pressed plaid pants of all colors and descriptions. I could not throw them away. The plaid pants reminded me of my dad, and I held on to a few pairs and imagined him wearing them and handing me a teddy bear, his first gift I recall receiving as a little girl. Unbelievably, I found a woman named Tammy who makes "Tammy Bears" from your loved one's clothing and is dedicated to giving comfort and warmth to people who wish to preserve a memory. I also learned that Tammy, an amazingly determined artist, was born with one hand. She persisted until she learned to stitch and sew, and these gorgeous love-out-loud bears now sit in my house, plus each of my grand-daughter's rooms and my daughter's. Tammy's bears are beyond remarkable, and she personalized mine with the name Honey.

Frame a family recipe. Perhaps your loved one was a great baker or cook and famous in your family for a recipe. Make copies and then frame the original, per-haps with a photograph of your loved one. Ensure that the recipe is handed down, and preserve it as an heir-loom. Let everyone chime in with ideas for naming it in your loved one's honor.

Save a favorite book. My mother was an avid reader even as a little girl. I inherited her copy of *Little Women*, which had a nameplate sticker in the inside cover that said, "This book belongs to Phyllis Blonder." It was given to my mom by my great-aunt Francie, who adored her. The year was 1938, and it continues to be one of my treasures.

Create a memorial garden. If your loved one loved plants, flowers, and gardening, consider donating funds for a garden in their name or planting one in their memory. It could be at a local park, at your place of worship, on the grounds of a volunteer organization that was special to your loved one, or even in your backyard. Donating a tree and planting it in the garden in another's honor is also a beautiful way to acknowledge them as the years go by.

Gift a circle of love. A loving father decided to give his two sons the ultimate Father's Day gift: the ring his dad had left him after he passed away. To do so, he had a mold created and the ring was duplicated to perfection. When his wife realized he now wouldn't have his father's ring, she surprised him and had another duplicate made so he could keep his father's original ring. The circle of love continued, and one day the rings would be handed down from his sons to each of their sons, his grandsons.

Create a wedding memory. At her daughter's wedding, one mother wanted to honor grandparents who had passed and had thumbnail photographs made into charms attached to ribbons incorporated into the bouquet. Another mom lost her mother weeks before her child's wedding and pinned a photograph inside a tiny pocket sewn into her dress.

Let photographs speak volumes. Surround yourself with photographs that speak to you. It's impossible to live with every photograph, so selecting the significant ones that tell a story is a way to cull them down to a special few. My friend Terry treasured a photo of her father at his college graduation because it was like he was looking after her. She added, "Throughout my life he was always worried about me, and to this day, I feel like his eyes in this picture are still watching over me."

Share a life story. At her daughter-in-law's baby shower, Judy Garfinkel, a devoted mom, welcomed the birth of her upcoming grandchild with a meaningful gift. She created a book for the baby with photographs of her son and titled it *Let Me Tell You about Your...Dad*. The book told her son's life story and was filled with details all about him. She included pictures of his artwork and school photographs from kindergarten through college. It was a touching, picture-perfect gift all about Daddy for the bundle of joy on the way.

Store and preserve photographs properly. Over time, if you frame and display everything, you'll have little room for anything but photographs. It helps to start saving pictures digitally and store backups in a few places, just in case. When saving fragile and precious photographs, be sure to consult experts on how to store them safely, away from degrading environmental conditions. Get professional help if you wish to preserve a special photograph, and avoid just throwing it in a box. If you have photographs to share with friends from your childhood, create a time capsule, and bring it out at momentous occasions.

The Writing's on the Wall

A loved one's handwriting is identifiable and memorable, and a greeting card, a valentine, or a letter will one day be a treasured gift. It becomes a special, "signature" keepsake and way to stay connected. While many documents might be typed, even a signed name can say "I love you." Here are some ways to preserve the handwriting of your parents or other family members who have passed:

Frame a letter. If you have received or have in your possession a letter that is sentimental or something you'd like to save, have it framed and preserved. When my mother and father married, my grandfather Irving wrote my father a letter, promising his support and love, while sharing his fond wishes for their marriage and a life of happiness together. My mother cherished that letter and kept it in her vault, and I eventually framed it. That letter was precious to my mother, who deeply loved her daddy.

Save greeting cards. Over the years, I've saved special greeting cards from my parents and children. Their sweet notes, words of affection, and fond wishes are a memory I want to preserve. I look at them often and feel the love inside those cards. I inherited this idea from my mother, who saved dozens of greeting cards. A special surprise was discovering the saved Valentine's, Mother's, and Father's Day cards I created for my parents when I was a little girl. Those homemade cards shared my love in poems I wrote and bring a smile many years later.

Write an ethical will. Ethical wills left in a vault or protected place become beloved heirlooms. An ethical will stipulates what you wish for family members and specific people you care about — what values you wish to share that you hope they continue to embody in their lives. The goal is to impart your beliefs, wisdom, and gratitude, leaving behind a powerful statement and affirmation of how much you loved someone. I have written letters to my children and update them every five to ten years so that they will be relevant. It's my hope that those letters will provide comfort, love, and endless "hugs" so that even when I'm not physically present, they'll know that I'm with them always.

> **LOL:** When you are touched by the words written by someone you care about, save them over time. Even handwriting can become an out-loud reminder of how we are loved.

Preparing a Eulogy

A eulogy is one of the hardest things to write and say. Yet it's one of life's bittersweet honors. To sum up someone's entire life in a eulogy is a daunting task. However, once you know you've given it your all and done it justice, your words will be infused with meaning and purpose. As you write a eulogy, consider your relationship with the deceased and get in touch with the stories, happy times, and most meaningful part of someone's life that can be shared.

Here are a few ways to get in touch with what matters as you write a eulogy:

- Think about what your loved one would want you to say. Get in touch with what they would want imparted to everyone at a funeral or tribute service. Would they want you to offer words inspiring others to make a difference? Love others more? Laugh more? Give more? Think about their soul and spirit, and share it out loud.

- Quote life lessons that your loved one said to you, lived by, and repeated often. Did they believe "To thine own self be true"? Or "Find the good in the bad, and be positive"? Share the essence of who they were and what they believed that can be passed on purposefully.

- Give comfort to those attending the service. Remember, everyone is there to share your loss and sadness.

• Inquire with the funeral home or cemetery if it is possible to tape your eulogy or stream it online for friends and family members who can't attend the services. A memorial is a very emotional time for everyone, and having an opportunity to reflect by listening to prayers and tributes can be very meaningful.

Expressing Meaningful Condolences to Others

Writing a note of condolence is a significant opportunity to commemorate someone's life and express your sympathies. Sharing your feelings can deeply touch the families of loved ones lost. Over the years, I have saved some of these expressions of condolences because they summed up my mother's or father's life with such heartfelt appreciation of their endless love, giving, and attention. When possible, write a condolence letter or send a card and donation without delay. Check to see if there's a nonprofit cause to which contributions have been requested or that would mean the most to a family.

Here are some things to keep in mind when writing a note to convey sorrow or paying a visit to someone who is grieving:

• Focus on life, not death. When someone dies, consider how you might communicate feelings about their value as an individual who brightened lives. Or focus on what a loving daughter, son, or caregiver that family member was and how their acts of loving-kindness inspired you. Reflect on how they lived and the love that surrounded them versus how they passed.

- Consider making a donation to a cause that mattered to the loved one, but take the time to share your feelings in a card or letter as well. Also, check back in on the bereaved weeks later, as they are still mourning and might need someone to talk to about their loss.

- When visiting family, be prepared to share a story about the person that illustrates how they helped you, what they meant to you, or a time when they did something meaningful that would resonate with loved ones.

- Avoid saying that you understand how someone else feels. Everyone's story is different, even when you've both nursed someone during illness or experienced a similar tragic loss. We can't be in each other's shoes, but we can share our deepest thoughts, show empathy, and say, "I'm so sorry for your loss." Say the deceased's name and personalize your feelings, especially if you knew the person well: "I loved Ben; he was such a friendly person and always had a smile on his face and a kind greeting when I saw him. He really knew how to make someone feel special."

Forever in Your Heart

While loved ones' birthdays, or the anniversaries of their deaths, are often sad reminders of those we love, they offer moments to memorialize someone and show how much that individual meant to us. These traditions keep their memory alive and close to our hearts, though their physical presence is gone. I still feel my parents with me as I continue to honor their lives in meaningful ways.

Here are a few ideas to keep your loved ones who have departed close:

A family gathering. A family who lost their matriarch gets together on her birthday and goes to her favorite drive-in hamburger restaurant. Everyone gathers for a graveside visit and then heads to the spot for their yearly ritual. Consider creating a tradition to honor your loved ones, even if you do something small throughout the year in their memory rather than making a big effort on a specific day. It's a way for loving hearts to stay in touch.

A just-because call. While I don't talk that often to my parents' friends or more distant relatives who meant so much to them, it makes me feel so good when I do reach out. When I call my mother's best friends to say hello or check in on them, I can feel my mom's gratitude and almost hear her praise telling me how wonderful that gesture was, and even in her absence, I can keep her spirit by my side. I know how much my call means, and this "just because" thoughtfulness goes a long, long ways.

A Grandma day. Proclaim a special day in honor of a parent or grandparent or friend. For example, if a grandmother loved to get her nails done or take a walk and sit on a particular park bench, treat the girls in the family to a day of remembrance celebrating her memory with these activities. Or if a relative loved to volunteer at a specific place, do so in their honor.

> **LOL:** Love does not die when a person dies. Your love for those you care about persists long after they are gone. Give a voice to the beauty of that relationship by sharing your love out loud.

Three LOL Things You Can Do Today to Cherish Loved Ones

1. **Consider what your legacy will be long after you are gone.** How will you be remembered? What causes or passions do you care most about? How do you want to be remembered? Think of your actions today and how they will shape those memories in the future. Share the things that matter most to you, and write an ethical will or letter to your children, or tape a video message expressing your love for your family members out loud.

2. **Preserve a loved one's legacy.** Whether it's framing medals of honor, protecting a Bible or book passed down through the generations, or paying tribute by naming something in memory of a loved one, think of a way to honor their life. Select one thing and give it a front-row placement in your life.

3. **Shift your to-do list to a "to-love list."** Reframe
    your daily action items by making a list of whom
    you can express loving-kindness to. Turn grief into
    giving by making a difference in the lives of others.
    Whether it's donating clothing from a loved one
    who has passed or a belonging that might help
    another person, consider ways to make your loss
    and love transformative. Select one cause that you
    feel your loved ones would embrace, and create
    a scholarship or make a donation in their honor.
    Keep their memory alive, and put your love-out-
    loud list in play.

CHAPTER 10

LOVE IN ACTION

I hope this little book will remind you of the power of our words, thoughts, and deeds. Love is action. We can tell someone we love them a thousand times, but when we show it and express it, even in little ways, we have a remarkable opportunity to spread positive energy into the world proactively.

If we all do one kind thing daily — share a word of praise, perhaps, or uplift another person in need — we can make the world a brighter place. By doing so, we make our own lives count, and our giving feels so good. We all have the potential to leave things better than we found them. To be a more loving version of ourselves. To remain calm and loving even during a storm. To lessen the suffering or pain or worries of another. This is *human kindness* at work and is, simply, the right thing to do.

Loving Out Loud provides a path and plan to help you accomplish this goal in greater measure. Offering an abundance of compassion and extending kindness are steps that visibly manifest love. Like the seeds in a beautiful flower garden, small intentions of goodness can be planted and take root wherever you go. You can leave behind a trail of light. Consider how love at first sight is more about how you love out loud. Even at first glance, if your heart is open to others, you are more able to receive happiness and love.

Falling in love with life, while accepting that it is filled with ups and downs, is an opportunity to share our strength and resilience. We all take some hits in life at times — it's just a matter of when — but it's then how we respond that ultimately defines us. Whenever possible, lean toward love.

When we turn our heads and look the other way when we see pain, hardship, or suffering, we diminish our own potential. When we avoid conflict because it's the easiest thing to do or confrontation is too hard, we miss an opportunity to make a difference. When we bury ourselves in technology and communicate impersonally, we lose our powerful human touch. We miss that special spark that our voice or a hug or high five gives to someone. Our brains and hearts need to experience love. The words of love. The demonstrations of love. The feelings that tell us we are cherished. When it comes to loving out loud, the playing field is level. We are equally able to give and receive it.

When I asked Eddie Mendel — a generous individual, cofounder of Ned Davis Research, and minority owner of the Atlanta Falcons — what inspires him most, he replied with some life-enhancing insights. He said, "I believe in being courteous. It's so easy to tell someone serving or helping you that you appreciate them." Eddie credited learning the importance of kindness from his father and also his grandfather. A few weeks before he passed away, his dad, Edwin Sr., was at the pharmacy and saw an elderly woman who was not able to afford her medication. He pulled out a hundred-dollar bill and paid for her medicine. When she gratefully asked who it was she had to thank for this generous act of kindness, he modestly replied, "My name is not important."

"What Have You Done for Mankind Today?"

The power of love and acts of kindness are well documented. Research has shown evidence of positive physical and mental health benefits from giving to others. When you let a little love in your heart, you are enhancing your life. When you give a little love from your heart, you are enhancing your life as well as those of others. Love allows you to share a piece of yourself. Unleashing those feelings can brighten the world and accelerates joy.

Love is not a trend. Loving-kindness is not a passé notion or relic of another time. We're all in this together. Upgrade the manner in which you express love. Love who you are. Love what you think, speak, and do.

A profound conversation I had after viewing a movie about Ben Ferencz's life led me to think further about the power of words and the focus of this book. I spoke with Ben's son, Don Ferencz. A world-renowned ninety-nine-year-old humanitarian lawyer, Ben Ferencz is one of the most respected voices in the field of international justice. Ben served as chief prosecutor for the United States at the Nuremberg trials following World War II and has spent his entire life working for world peace and to protect human rights.

Don's poignant story about growing up as Ben's son summed it all up and inspired me: "My dad always said, 'Don't leave a place the way you found it; leave it the way you would like to have found it.' He led and taught by example. Each night at dinner, my father would go around the table asking each of his four children in turn, 'What have you done for mankind today?'"

Don shared:

My mom taught us how to set the table and iron our own clothes, but what could we, as

young children, really tell him beyond our little deeds? We didn't necessarily have great answers as children, but we grew up in a house
that had an indoctrination to teach us to think
broadly and help others. My sister and I later
marched in New York City with Martin Luther
King, and my entire life has been dedicated
to human rights and promoting world peace.
This one question was so routine that I'll never
forget it, and I work toward making a difference, having majored in Peace and Conflict
Studies at Colgate University. The point of
his dinner-table question was clear. We can all
make a difference.

Inspired by Don's father's question, I asked my
four- and six-year-old granddaughters, who were staying with us while their parents were out of town, "What
have you done for humankind today?" Their first question was "What is humankind?" As I explained that
humankind is all of us in the world, a lightbulb went
off, and since they had spoken at home about helping others and kindness, the girls proudly shared their
day's good deed.

The next night at dinner, before I could get to the
question, Dani, the six-year-old, asked me what I'd done
for humankind that day. I smiled and answered. A few
days later when I saw Dani again, she repeated the question: "What have you done for humankind today?"

Be an Ambassador of Love

In the spirit of these words, conversations and the self-less acts by dedicated souls who have stood up against wrongdoing and unfair treatment and indecencies in life, let's continue to ask the question of ourselves and future generations: "What have you done for human-kind today?" What will the conversation around your dinner table be? Please join in advancing the mission of a humankind filled with unstoppable kindness and help build a world of caring and compassion.

Be an "Ambassador of Love" and a blessing to oth-ers in life. Do not resist the joy and wisdom that come from sharing a generous spirit and a full heart and helping those in need.

We each have the ability to turn the key in the ig-nition of love. And if by chance your words inspire someone to share more love, then together this chain reaction has the power to catapult us toward the best of us. Feelings of isolation can disappear, and loneli-ness can fade. That's the power of loving out loud. We can all do better, starting with stepping-stones, which will become milestones. And everyone around you will know you stand for and stand up for love.

Say it out loud. Ask for the love you want; envi-sion and nurture the love you wish to grow. Live your life like a love song; after all, loving life is what it's all about. *Love is a many-splendored thing. Love will keep us together. I will always love you.* Make love your theme song. Love is not a passive pursuit. It's the ability to put yourself out there and share what's in your heart.

Create Your Best Life

As this book comes to a close, I hope you'll join me in pursuing a love-filled life, adding yourself to the guest list of an LOL celebration. Reflect every day on how you will build connections with others. By loving out loud, you have the opportunity and power within you to create a life without regrets. Loving out loud helps take you to a higher, more spiritual level of living.

It's no secret and is available to us all. Look for ways to infuse each day with vibrations of kindness, thoughtfulness, and concern for others. Do this by taking care of yourself — your emotional and physical health — and take small steps to bring out the best version of yourself. It takes a conscious awareness, focusing on what's beautiful in life. Be aware of all the good, caring deeds you can do, and realize how when you make an impact on another person's life, you ultimately enrich your own.

Sign each day with a signature style of love. Why? Because you care. Because you elected not to judge others. Because you didn't participate in a senseless argument. Because you didn't preach perfection or exude unrealistic expectations. Because you acted on a positive thought and let go of a negative one. Because you resisted hurting another's feelings and noticed someone else in need of a kind word or help. Any one of these would make for an amazing, awesome, loving-out-loud day.

Please help create a warm and loving life. Share this book with others who love you out loud. Say "thank you." Peel back the layers of anonymity, the mask of disinterest, and reveal a little more about yourself. Take a chance on love. Make a new friend. Help create a world that sits on the side of decency and goodness. Make yours a life that matters. Be the world to someone. Love madly; give passionately; and remind yourself to suffuse your life and those around you with meaning, magic, and immeasurable joy.

And last, *show* up, *lift* up, and never *give* up. Adopt a heart that is open and wise, and put out an LOL welcome mat. Take a deep breath and feel the gratitude for all that you appreciate now. There's no limit to what love can accomplish, especially if you share it freely. Let today be a wake-up call for how quickly everything can change. In the blink of an eye, life happens. Stay awake, enjoy the ride, and above all, love out loud.

ACKNOWLEDGMENTS

I am indebted to so many, who have generously shared their love, friendship, and guidance throughout my life. They are the kindhearted souls who lift me up and fill my life with joy.

To my beloved parents of blessed memory, Phyllis and Jack Freedman. Not a day goes by without your steadfast love. To my husband, Ed, my rock and love of my life, you make my life complete. To our children and grandchildren, I am so blessed to be a part of your lives and am deeply proud of you: Justin and Jaime,

Dani and Bella Spizman, Ali and Marc and Poppy Garfinkel, Randi Gerson, Jeff and Jack Gerson, Lee and Alicia, and Scott and Jordan Gerson. To my beloved aunt Lois Blonder; to my sisters and brothers-in-law, Doug and Genie Freedman, Esther and Mike Levine, and Cheryl Tuttle and Henry Frommer; to my devoted friend Bettye Storne; and to my extended family and friends, I cherish you all.

To my amazing literary agent, Meredith Bernstein. You have generously and skillfully shown up and supported me from the very start, out loud. Your steadfast devotion, unwavering encouragement, and thoughtful friendship brighten my world. You go far beyond what's expected, and because of your vision and bright ideas, this book became a reality. I am indebted to you.

To my New World Library team: Georgia Hughes, my skillful editor, who made writing this book an author's dream. Because of you, this book became magic. Your heartfelt insights and edits lifted my words to a new level, and your steadfast belief in bettering the world led the way. I am especially fortunate to work with you. Also, my gratitude to Alexandra Freemon, copy editor extraordinaire; Tracy Cunningham, art director; Kristen Cashman, managing editor; Tona Pearce Myers, production director; and Kim Corbin, senior publicist. I'm one lucky girl to be in such talented company and work with the best of the best.

I also owe thanks to the many individuals I have had the pleasure of working with, as they are giants in the literary, psychological, and business worlds. My dear friend H. Jackson Brown Jr., who wrote the *New York Times* bestselling *Life's Little Instruction Book*, have I thanked you today? To Drs. Marianne and Stephen Garber, for your lifelong friendship. To the amazing Tory Johnson, for teaming up with me to help women at work; and Edie Fraser, who lives by and inspired "Do your giving while you are living." To my son Justin Spizman, exceptional writer and lawyer, for encouraging the book on Jimmy V's speech, which inspired a nation, and the list goes on.

Two thumbs-up also go to purpose leader extraordinaire Joey Reiman, with whom I was fortunate to work for many years. To my pal Bruce T. Blythe, for your endless wisdom in life; Rick Frishman, for our Author 101 adventures; Tony Conway, who said yes when I reentered the corporate world; Michael Greenbaum, for your generosity and goodness; and Dr. Warren Woodruff, who fills my life with classical music, joy, and purpose.

My additional gratitude goes to the following friends, family members, and experts who inspired me. Thank you, one and all, from the bottom of my heart: Dr. Eva Arkin, Marcy Aronow and Fred Katz, Spring Asher, Ellen Banov, Lindsay Berg, Sara Blaine and Mendel Rotenberg, Suzanne Blonder, Rick Blue, PhD, Perla and Miles Brett, Georgia Brown, Patty and Larry Brown, Bob Burg, Ken Byers, Tena Clark, Jay Cohen, Steve Cohen, Jan Collins, Sharon Corenblum,

Christine Crowton, Joey DeBlasi, Stevie Doughty,
Julia Doyle, Dale Dyer, Emily Einstein, Robert Faneuil,
Bobby Feirman, Ben Ferencz, Don Ferencz, Nancy
Freedman, Sally Freedman, Viki Freeman, Brenda and
Ken Fritz, Barbara and David Garber, DDS, Judy and
David Garfinkel, Leon Goldstein, Ronald Goldstein,
DDS, Norma Gordon, Tracy Green, Anne and Michael
Greenbaum, Stuart Gustafson, James, Eva, and Angelica
Hale, Erik Hedrick and Bryan Kirkland, Rabbi Joshua
Heller, Tammy Hendricks, Gail Heyman, Scott Heyman,
Arlene Hoffman, Emily Hutmacher, Cheryl Isaacs,
Leslie Isenberg, Dr. David Jacobson, Marcia Jaffe, Lisa
Karesh, Susanne Katz, Cheryl Kortemeier, Amanda
Leesburg, Shira Levine, Anthony Levitas, PhD, Lorie
Lewis, Ron Lipsitz, Carla and Ralph Lovell, Jo Mathisen,
Harry Mazier, Ryan McEntyre, Eddie Mendel, Dr.
Howard Miller, Diana and John Milner, Melisa Morrow,
Jack Morton, Joey and Susie Moskowitz, Fran and
Bob Penn, Angie Perry, Dr. Michael Popkin, Christine
Pullara Newton, Linda Reisman, Harriette Reznik,
Maxine Rosen, Evie Sacks and Cary Rodin, Keith Saks,
Rabbi Neil Sandler, the Sandy Springs Society, Leigh
and Michael Schiff, Laurie Selzer, Jason Sherman, Lori
Simon, Terry Spector, Lynn Stallings, Keisha Stanley,
Molly Stryer, Tom Sullivan, Linda Sulvasky, Helen
Taffet, Shade Taylor, Carol Tuchman, Chris von Seeger,
Germaine and Bruce Weinstein, Donna Weinstock,
Ava Wilensky, Donna Wilensky, Jay Wilson, David and
Deborah Woodsfellow, and Amy Sacks Zeide.

NOTES

Chapter 1. Start Right, Stay Right

Page 6, *In every case, happiness (and distress) comes from within*: Bruce T. Blythe, email interview with the author, March 3, 2019.

Page 20, *Using our five senses as often as possible*: Steve Ochoa, email and telephone conversation with the author, April 19, 2019.

Page 22, *A laser-sharp insight came from Scott*: Gail Heyman, email and telephone conversation with the author, March 11, 2019.

Chapter 2. Have I Thanked You Today?

Page 28, *Often…our own light goes out, and is rekindled*: Albert Schweitzer, "The Dignity of the Individual," in *Albert Schweitzer: An Anthology*, ed. Charles R. Joy (Boston: The Beacon Press, 1947), 153.

Chapter 3. Inspiring Your Partner to Love You Out Loud

Page 53, *Kind, loving words are one of the easiest ways*: David Woodsfellow, email and telephone conversation with the author, March 3, 2019.

Chapter 4. Raising Kinder Children

Page 77, *If I were to suggest something I've noticed*: Bob Burg, email to the author, August 20, 2018.

Page 80, *The way to be successful in a complex world*: Joey Reiman, telephone and email conversation with the author, April 23, 2019.

Page 83, *It was 1994, and I was watching the news*: Amy Sacks Zeide, email interview with the author, April 10, 2019.

Page 93, *one teen honored fallen soldiers by writing their names*: "Teen Dons Patriotic Prom Dress to Honor 25 Fallen Soldiers," *Inside Edition*, April 30, 2019, https://www.insideedition.com/teen-dons-patriotic-prom-dress-honor-25-fallen-soldiers-52576.

Chapter 5. Loving Your Friends Out Loud

Page 103, *doing your giving while you are living*: Edie Fraser, email to the author, January 21, 2019.

Page 104, *I lost a dear friend, who was also my patient*: Dr. Howard Miller, email to the author, January 30, 2019.

Page 109, *When it comes to my friends*: Christine Pullara, telephone and email conversation with the author, January 21, 2019.

Page 116, *When you share your feelings with a friend*: Maxine Rosen, conversation and email with the author, January 2019.

Page 122, *I'm so blessed that my daughters are best friends*: Christine Pullara, email to the author, January 21, 2019.

Chapter 6. Bonding with Your Family

Page 130, *When it comes to family, keep in mind*: Anthony Levitas, PsyD, email interview with the author, February 13, 2019.

Page 133, *We tell our kids and family members*: Brenda Fritz, telephone conversation with the author, February 2019.

Page 135, *My first and brightest influence*: Christine Pullara, email to the author, January 25, 2019.

Page 137, *As a family we strive to create a loving atmosphere*: Marianne Daniels Garber, PhD, email to the author, February 26, 2019.

Page 138, *On Lorraine Fleishman's ninetieth birthday*: Cheryl Isaacs, email to the author, March 14, 2019.

Page 139, *My childhood friend Gail*: Gail Heyman, interview with the author, March 11, 2019.

Page 144, *A devoted mom named Gennie*: Gennie Handmaker, email to the author, January 10, 2019.

Page 151, *When Marcia, a dedicated grandmother*: Marcia Jaffe, telephone and email conversation with the author, February 14, 2019.

Page 157, *We all (male and female, siblings and parents) should do DNA testing*: Robert Faneuil, conversation and email with the author, February 14, 2019.

Chapter 7. Loving Out Loud at Work,
by Volunteering, and On the Go

Page 165, *Make a loving, not a living*: Joey Reiman, telephone and email conversation with the author, April 23, 2019.

Page 166, *here's a sampling of Shira's Top Ten*: Shira Levine, email to the author, February 15, 2019.

Page 167, *There's a prominent place for kindness in business*: Harry Maziar, email to the author, February 4, 2019.

Page 168, *I learned about her father, Bill Savitt*: Spring Asher, email to the author, February 9, 2019.

Page 176, *Giving is important because it's something that we all need*: Emily Hutmacher, email to the author, February 5, 2019.

Page 181, *Because it feels damn good*: Ken Byers, email to the author, February 6, 2019.

Page 183, *Kindness in the workplace goes a long way*: Cheryl Kortemeier, email to the author, February 14, 2019.

Page 184, *When I see suffering, I have to do something*: Michael and Anne Greenbaum, emails to the author, February 7, 2019.

Page 185, *The best recognition I ever received*: Linda (who prefers not to be identified by last name), conversation with the author, February 14, 2019.

Page 189, *When Dr. Peter Gordon retired*: Norma Gordon, email to the author, February 7, 2019.

Chapter 8. Creating Love-Out-Loud
Moments and Gifts

Page 195, *Hal David was a huge inspiration in my career*: Tena Clark, email to the author, February 14, 2019.

Page 196, *Teaching another human being the artful craft of music*: Dr. Warren Woodruff, email to the author, February 15, 2019.

Page 200, *I have the pleasure of working with someone*: Christine Pullara, email to the author, January 21, 2019.

Page 203, *he bends over backward and would stand on his head*: Spring Asher, conversation with the author, February 19, 2019.

Page 218, *For my birthday, my partner, Bryan, gave me*: Erik Hedrick, conversation with the author, February 14, 2019.

Page 219, *A pair of brothers get together*: Bob Penn, conversation with the author, December 4, 2019.

Chapter 9. Cherishing Loved Ones and Preserving Memories

Page 230, *When my friend Julie's husband died*: Jan Collins, email to the author, February 6, 2019.

Page 233, *At her daughter-in-law's baby shower*: Judy Garfinkel, email to the author, April 20, 2019.

Chapter 10. Love in Action

Page 245, *I believe in being courteous*: Eddie Mendel, email to the author, January 21, 2019.

Page 246, *My dad always said*: Don Ferencz, telephone conversation and email interview with the author, February 26, 2019.

ABOUT THE AUTHOR

Robyn Spizman is an award-winning, *New York Times* bestselling author and veteran media personality who has appeared often on NBC's *Today* show. She appears frequently on television (especially the Atlanta NBC affiliate WXIA's *Atlanta & Company*), on radio broadcasts and podcasts, at live events, and in print as an expert at choosing and giving gifts and for other lifestyle segments. A consummate organizer and networker, she works regularly with national corporations and nonprofits as a keynote speaker and to create events and fund-raisers. She has been named Georgia's Author of the Year and A Diva in Business and has received numerous other awards for her writing and leadership acumen. She lives in Atlanta, Georgia, with her husband, Ed, and is a devoted mother, grandmother, and community volunteer. Visit her website at www.robynspizman.com.